CW01464538

ISBN 978-1-330-28447-6
PIBN 10013162

1 MONTH OF
FREE
READING

at

www.ForgottenBooks.com

By purchasing this book you are eligible for one month membership to ForgottenBooks.com, giving you unlimited access to our entire collection of over 700,000 titles via our web site and mobile apps.

To claim your free month visit:

www.forgottenbooks.com/free13162

Similar Books Are Available from
www.forgottenbooks.com

DOMESTIC LIFE IN SCOTLAND, 1488–1688

A SKETCH OF THE DEVELOPMENT OF FURNITURE AND HOUSEHOLD USAGE

(Rhind Lectures in Archæology, 1919–20)

BY

JOHN WARRACK

WITH SIXTEEN ILLUSTRATIONS

NEW YORK
E. P. DUTTON AND COMPANY
PUBLISHERS

PREFACE

FEW realise how modern are the conceptions of comfort and decency which inspire the furnishing and arrangements of our present-day homes, or how different were the conditions in which, only a few centuries ago, our forefathers spent their lives. Till the beginning of the seventeenth century chairs for ordinary household use were unknown. Hats were worn at meals. Washing formed no part of the morning toilet, even in Charles II's time, and very few in any country in Europe washed their faces every day. The use of forks did not become general till the eighteenth century, and food was picked from the general dish and raised to the mouth with the fingers.

The development of Domestic Life has not, I think, hitherto been studied as a continuous process, nor traced to its social and historical origins, though many of its details have been worked out and much knowledge of a fragmentary kind has been accumulated. In trying to reconstruct the domestic life of Scotland at various epochs in the fifteenth, sixteenth and seventeenth centuries, and to trace the lines of development, I have had recourse to the comparison and analysis of many hundreds of early inventories which are to be found among the national documents preserved in the Register House, and the study of these records has resulted in much new and curious information as to the details of household life in early times. I have also drawn freely on early Scottish literature, including biographies, journals and account books, for material likely to put my readers into more living touch with the men, women and children of the times with which I have dealt.

While the book deals mainly with Scotland, there are many references to the social development of England, France and other countries in western Europe. For a general enquiry there is a certain advantage in the smaller and less crowded stage. To the non-Scottish reader I would address the invitation and guarantee given by a character in a witty French comedy :—

Mon camarade
Allons faire au jardin un tour de promenade !
Suivez-moi sans rien craindre ; il est dans mes principes
De ne forcer personne à louer nos tulipes !

To express in detail all my obligations to those who have helped me would overweight my book. But I must acknowledge the kindness of Sir James Balfour Paul, C.V.O., in reading my proofs ; of Mr. F. C. Eeles in advising me as to the contents of the Oratory in the second Lecture ; of Prof. Hannay and Dr. Hay Fleming ; and of Dr. Thomas Ross, Dr. William Kelly, A.R.S.A., Aberdeen, and

Mr. James Beveridge, Linlithgow. My best thanks are also due to those who have allowed me to reproduce articles in their possession among my illustrations.

13 ROTHESAY TERRACE
    EDINBURGH

CONTENTS

LECTURE IV

THE DECAY OF FEUDALISM AND THE DEVELOPMENT OF FAMILY LIFE

JAMES VI, 1578–1625

New conceptions of domestic life—Historical origins of the change—Passing away of feudalism—Expansion of trade and increasing importance of the towns—Enrichment of the nobles by partition of Church property—An era of building—Domestic character of the new architecture—Feudal lords transformed into courtiers, with luxurious standards of living—Changes in domestic arrangements—The hall gives place to the dining-room—The " Dravand Buird "—Table manners at Court and in private life—Table ware, etc. Display of plate—Cupboards with " gries "—The dresser—Dessert and the banquet—The parlour — Stuffed chairs — The taffel — Books : the Family Bible — Pictures — Music — Life of the leisured classes—Men's employments and

regime—History of the times reflected in furniture—Severe and utilitarian character of Commonwealth furniture—Restoration chairs and day-beds—Chairs as evidences of changes in the treatment of floors—Easy chairs—Extravagance of the Court—Exotic materials—Cabinets—The chest of drawers—Tea, coffee and cocoa—Walnut tables—The virginalls—Barred grates—Forks not yet in use—Scottish diarists—Social life of the time—Billiards—Horse racing—The kirk stool—Going to church—Giving out the line—The hourglass—Periwigs, powder and Sedan chairs, as preluding the eighteenth century—Conclusion

LIST OF ILLUSTRATIONS

NOTE.—The Illustrations from Holyrood are by permission
of the King, to whom the copyright belongs.

DOMESTIC LIFE IN SCOTLAND
1488-1688

LECTURE I

IN FEUDAL DAYS: A MEDIÆVAL CASTLE

THE FIFTEENTH CENTURY

Poverty of the country—Unsettled conditions—Scarcity of native timber—Foreign trade: exports and imports—Inferences as to social conditions in Scotland and in Flanders—Value of knowledge of early social life in interpreting early literature—The mediæval castle and its furnishings—An evening meal—Washing the hands—Early codes of manners and rules for behaviour—Table arrangements—The salt-fatt, dishes, spoons, and serviotts—Arrangements and furnishing of the hall—" Till necessitie and nocht til decore "—The dais—The hie burde—Literary references—The parelling—The comptar or counter: origin and line of development—The chalmer of des: its position and uses—Bedrooms—Beds and canopies—The futegang.

IF, among the nations of Europe, Scotland has played but a humble part in the development of design in furniture, the facts of nature and of history at least supply a simple explanation. A high standard of domestic comfort is the outcome of a long experience of national prosperity, and the sure index of a well established social order. Now it is true that, in intellectual culture, Scotland had reached even in mediæval times

a level which, considering her scattered population and her meagre opportunities, is remark
able.   But if her reputation in letters was
secure, so alas was her poverty proverbial.
" What   could   have   brought   us   hither ? "
asked the French knights who, as Froissart
tells us, had come over in 1385 to march against
England ; " we have never known till now what
was meant by poverty and hard living ! "   It
would be easy to collect similar testimonies
from those who have left records of their
journeyings in Scotland, but the task would
be both dismal and unnecessary.   Some of
these writers speak of the Scots with kindliness,
some with contempt ; but there is hardly one
among them who has not recorded some impression of the poverty of the country.   Some
hundreds of years ago it was a current jibe in
France that when the Devil led our Lord into
a high mountain and showed him all the king-
doms of the earth and the glory thereof, he
thought it discreet to make one reservation.
He " keipit his meikle thoomb on Scotland."

But besides being a poor country, Scotland
was also a singularly unsettled one.   By a
misfortune of geography it was her richest
provinces that lay exposed to the devastating
raids from the English border.   History too
brought her mischances.   The long series of
regencies during the minorities of the Jameses

gave rise to bitter jealousies and family feuds among the nobles ; and from the consequences of these factions and the social anarchy they brought in their train, not even the most peaceable country folk could count themselves secure. " Sum time," says Lyndsay of the Mount ·

> Sum time the realme was reulit be Regentis,
> Sum time lufetenantis, ledaris of the law ;
> Than rang sa mony inobedientis
> That few or nane stude of ane other aw ;
> Oppression did sa lowd hys bugle blaw
> That nane durst ride bot into feir of weir ;
> Jok-upon-land that time did mis his meir."

This is no fancy picture. Jok-upon-land, the decent peasant extorting a precarious living from an unkindly soil, was but too often a sufferer from the violence of the times. The records of actions for restoration of " spuilzie " not only tell us of such lawless deeds done by one noble to another, but they are full of petty and ruthless damage done to poor people who had little to lose. We read of attacks on richly furnished houses, and we have but to turn the page to find some poor Jok-upon-land complaining of " scaitht to his horse," another bent on recovering " auchteen pence takyn furth of hys purs," and a third claiming a still smaller sum for " hys wyfis hois and schone " ; while the august pages of the *Acta Dominorum Concilii* have embalmed for us the memory of " ane callit Cutsy," of whom only this has come down to us, that in a bitter hour four hundred and thirty years ago, he, or possibly she, suffered the " wrangous, violent and maisterful spoliatioun of twa sarkis."

To us these acts of oppression bring this compensation, that as the law required that the pursuer in an action for restitution should set forth under oath " the avail and quantitie of the gudis," we have a series of documents giving details and valuations of household gear in early times, of which we should otherwise have had but scanty record. Yet we cannot but realise as we read them, what tragedies of domestic life they describe, tragedies none the less moving that their scale is sometimes so pitifully small. They bring home to us that, for rich and poor alike, life was at the mercy of shocks and dislocations of every kind. Neither for life nor for property was there any security. And we must acknowledge that, in conditions so unsettled, it was hardly possible that there should be any equable and progressive development of the arts of peace.

Even if conditions had, however, been otherwise more favourable, Scotland would still have been at a disadvantage in the matter of furniture owing to her comparative dearth of fine timber. Not that Scotland was the treeless waste that some would have us believe. There was a fair amount of oak in the neighbourhood of Inver-

ness, as we know from the early records of that
town, while the forest of Badenoch produced
quantities of fir trees. Artillery wheels for the
raid of Norham were made in Melrose wood ;
timber was got at the same time from Clydes-
dale and the wood of Cockpen ; while James IV
used to send messengers to the Forest of Tern-
way, or Darnaway, in Morayshire, to " ger fell
tymmir " there. We have particulars, too, of
timber felled at Luss, and elsewhere in the
neighbourhood of Loch Lomond, in connection
with the King's barge, built at Dumbarton in
1494. Still, the visitor who had passed through
England could not but be struck with the
comparative scarcity of trees in Scotland ; and
though Nicander Nucius, writing in 1545,
states that the *whole island* abounds with
marshes and well-timbered oak forests, it is
questionable whether his journey actually extended to Scotland. We know that, as a matter
of fact, Scotland depended mainly on her imports of " eastland burdis " from the Baltic ;
and it is safe to conclude that Scotland was
poorly supplied with timber, though not to the
extent suggested by Sir Anthony Weldon when
he said that " had Christ been betrayed in this
country, Judas had sooner found the grace of
repentance than a tree to hang himself on."

But any preliminary survey of the conditions
affecting Scottish domestic life and its equip-

ment would be incomplete and wholly misleading if it did not look beyond the boundaries
of the country itself. Even in mediæval times
Scotland cannot be considered as existing " in
vacuo," or as insulated from foreign contacts.
We must have some idea of how social conditions in Scotland compared with those ruling
elsewhere, and particularly in those countries
with which she had intimate relations ; and we
must know something of the channels through
which the influences of countries with a more
highly organised social and domestic life were
conveyed to her. Even in England the standard
of domestic comfort was, up to the end of the
fifteenth century, much lower than in the principal countries on the continent of Europe.
Indeed, even fifty years later, the Spaniards
are said to have remarked, " These English
have their houses made of sticks and dirt, but
they fare commonly so well as the King." In
the last quarter of the fifteenth century, however, there was a clear advance towards comfort
and elegance in house equipment, and furniture
of some artistic pretension began to be introduced. For guidance in such matters England
naturally looked to France and Flanders, and
there was, in fact, little important furniture in
England which was not either of foreign origin
or at least of foreign inspiration. It need
hardly be said that Scotland, with her smaller

population, her poorer communities and her ruder material civilisation, was even more dependent on her contact with foreign countries for an advancing standard of domestic comfort and artistic seemliness. Fortunately we have, in the Ledger of Andrew Halyburton, an authoritative document as to Scottish trade with the Netherlands in the closing years of the fifteenth century. Halyburton was an enterprising Scottish commission merchant, established at Middelburg, and doing business also at Bruges, Antwerp and elsewhere ; and his clientèle included many leading churchmen and laymen in Scotland, as well as many of the tradesmen who supplied goods to the Royal Household. An examination of his Ledger shows that the exports from Scotland consisted almost entirely of unmanufactured products ; a few bales of Scottish cloth seem to be the only exception. The bulk of the trade is in skins, wool and fish, and even these do not always arrive in creditable condition. It must be confessed that the exports give a disappointing picture of the productiveness and industry of the country, and we have to correct this impression by reminding ourselves that most of the necessaries and some of the luxuries for home consumption were produced by native industry.

The imports from Flanders are much more

various and interesting, and they may be examined in more detail because of the light they throw on the social life of the time. We are struck at once, for instance, with the large proportion of dress materials, velvets and damasks, silks and satins, as well as humbler stuffs such as " ryssillis cloth," buckram and fustian. At first sight this seems inconsistent with the idea of Scotland's poverty ; but we may recall Pedro de Ayala's contemporaneous statement that the people of Scotland spent all they had to keep up appearances, and were as well dressed as it was possible to be in such a country. It must be kept in mind too that a mediæval conception of society regulated the laws of costume ; and the demand for costly materials is to some extent explained by the fact that they had a definite significance in announcing the rank and social importance of the wearer.

Next to the trade in dress materials comes that in groceries, spices and wines, and the variety of these shows a rather more luxurious standard of living than we might have expected. There was, for instance, a demand for olives, as well as for figs, almonds, raisins and dates, and for spices and confections of many kinds ; while there are frequent puncheons of " claret Gas chœo," " Mawvyssie " and other wines, including some from the Rhine. Next may be mentioned the trade in church and domestic furnishings, a trade which considerably increased in the following century, but was meanwhile of no great volume   To its details I must return later. Another interesting import consists of illuminated books, chiefly porteuses and breviaries, and there are occasional shipments of a ream or half ream of paper. It will be noticed that in all that has been enumerated there is little that is not destined for immediate use. If we look for materials for work to be done in Scotland, we find little beyond madder, for dyeing ; some iron, for smith-work ; gunpowder, carts and wheelbarrows for quarrying and building ; white and red lead and vermilion, and gold and silver foil, probably for decoration of churches and other buildings ; and sewing silks for embroidery.

Now consider for a moment what is implied in the contrast between the exports from Scotland and the imports from Flanders. Scotland, as we have seen, exported practically nothing but fish, wool and skins—fish speared or netted in her lochs and rivers and estuaries ; wool sheared from the sheep on her hillsides and lowland pastures ; skins of animals shot or snared in her mountains or forests. Thus the whole outward foreign trade of Scotland was based, not on the organised industry of c. nmunities of skilled craftsmen and workers, but

on the primeval callings of the fisherman, the
shepherd and the huntsman ! In how different
a social atmosphere such a country must have
lived from that of one able to send out
immense quantities of tapestries, carved furniture, vessels of silver and gold, and fruits,
spices and wines, to every part of Europe. We
must, of course, make a fair allowance for the
fact that the Netherlands was a clearing-house
for European and extra-European trade. It is
something that Scotland was even importing
such artistic and other luxuries as Flanders
was able to supply ; and it is at least a tribute
to Scottish enterprise that these imports were
brought in Scottish vessels, commanded and
manned by Scotsmen. But it can readily be
seen that very little furniture, unless of a rough
and merely serviceable kind, was likely to be
made in Scotland, and that anything appealing
to a more sophisticated taste would be introduced from countries having a more highly
developed standard of design and workmanship. This further lesson may be drawn from
the facts we have been reviewing, that it would
be misleading to transfer to Scotland any
general picture of mediæval life which we may
have formed from accounts based on conditions
elsewhere. Such accounts are usually drawn
from the literature of countries with a
wealthy and elaborate civilisation ; from

illuminated manuscripts, highly coloured
fabliaux, and finely wrought interiors by
primitif painters, and they are apt to convey an impression that is overcharged and,
in its total effect, untrue, even of life in
those favoured lands. It would be unreasonable to expect to find in Scotland—a country so
poor, so unsettled and so isolated—any such
development of the material setting of social
life as existed in Italy, with her splendid artistic
traditions ; in Flanders, with her world-wide
commerce ; or in France, with her natural
taste and the luxury of her brilliant court.

Of Scottish Furniture of the fifteenth century
little or nothing remains ; nor have we any
contemporary illustration to turn to for information. But just because, in the absence of such
material, the subject has been neglected, it is
worth while to collect such knowledge as we
can derive from literary and documentary
sources and to form an idea of mediæval
practice in house-furnishing, and of the social
usages on which it was founded. Early
Scottish poetry is full of allusions to the
arrangements of domestic life, and unless we
have some acquaintance with these arrangements the allusions must remain obscure,
instead of casting a homely light on the poet's
thought. It is the more necessary because,
while the mediæval tradition persisted during

the changes of the sixteenth century, it disappeared altogether in the beginning of the seventeenth, and the very words used to describe once-familiar pieces of furniture and traditional domestic arrangements either acquired a new meaning or dropped completely out of the language. It was not till two hundred years later, during the Romantic Revival which originated, I suppose, with Horace Walpole and which led up to Sir Walter Scott, that there was a movement to recover a knowledge of mediæval customs and to exhume the lost vocabulary. As we shall see, the editors who at that time reprinted early Scottish poems were often puzzled by words and allusions which would have been intelligible had they known more of mediæval life, and they were too apt to tamper light-heartedly with the text, so that they sometimes introduced astonishing anachronisms. Even the pronunciation of forgotten words was a matter of mere guesswork, and the word " dais," which we pronounce to-day in two syllables, is an instance of such ignorance. In early times in this country it was a monosyllable, as it still is in France.

Let us see, therefore, what was the actual furnishing of a Scottish Castle in the latter part of the fifteenth century. Arriving at one of these strongholds in the dusk of a winter afternoon,

PLATE II

we are led up the winding stone staircase by a retainer swinging a horn lantern. On the first floor is the great hall, an apartment some thirty feet long, or more, in which the evening meal is about to be served. On one side a great fire of turf and peat burns in the wide fireplace, where there is, of course, no barred grate, and casts a ruddy glow through the room. A lad stands holding a metal basin, and the guests wash in turn, water from a laver or ewer being poured over their hands by another servant. A long narrow table is set across one end of the room, and at this the principal persons, some six or eight in number, take their seats with their backs to the wall. This table is known as the " hie burde," and it stands on a dais some inches higher than the rest of the floor, being reserved for the use of the more important guests. On the wall behind them is a piece of tapestry,[1] or a simpler hanging of coloured worsted. The lord of the castle sits in a high-backed chair[2] in the middle, and if he observes great state, there may be a canopy suspended from the ceiling above his seat. On his right and left are the guests seated on benches provided with loose cushions, and sometimes with "bancours" of tapestry or other woven material. The less important members of the household are seated at side tables, and they too have their

[1] See Plate III.   [2] See Plate II.

backs to the wall, so that the opposite side of each table is left free for service from the middle of the room. All those seated at the meal have their heads covered, the ladies, according to Scottish fashion, wearing kerchiefs draped from a high structure of real or false hair in the form of two horns—a dress which the Spanish ambassador described as the handsomest in the world. Only the servants are uncovered. The reason for wearing hats at meals seems to have been that it was considered a precaution against the contamination of the food by what a plain-spoken old writer calls " flyes and other fylthe." Our present standards of cleanliness and decency were not reached in a day, and a frank account of some of the table manners of the fifteenth century would fill us with disgust. Even in France people had to be warned that it was bad manners to spit or blow the nose at meals without turning aside the head ; that one must not struggle to catch fleas at table, nor seek to relieve the irritation of a then prevalent scalp-disease by scratching the head.

The table is spread with fair Dornick cloth, a diapered linen first made at Tournai, the same town which the Dutch called Dornewyk. Lighted candles stand on the tables and there are others in the chandillars of brass which hang from the roof On the table itself the most

TAPESTRY PANEL. (FIFTEENTH CENTURY) SHOWING CHILDREN'S GAMES

notable object is the salt-fatt, or salt-cellar, often
of elaborate design and considerable size. It
had a quasi-ceremonial importance, and servants were instructed that after the cloth was
laid they must first see that the salt cellar was in
place ; after that the knives, then the bread,
and last of all the food. The division of the
table into " above and below the salt " is not a
mediæval one, for those who were socially inferior sat at separate tables. Pewter dishes were
in fairly common use, but even in many important Scottish houses the old wooden trenchers
were not yet displaced. If there were a shortage
of plates, some of the retainers might have to
use slices of bread to hold their food. The
spoons were of pewter or occasionally of silver.
Knives are seldom mentioned in early inventories, because it was customary to use the
knives which men carried about with them for
general use. Forks were unknown and food
was carried to the mouth by the fingers. Politeness required that only three fingers, that is two
fingers and the thumb, should be used in
handling food ; and in drinking, the cup was
to be lifted in the same way. This handling of
food, and especially the fact that it was lifted
from the general dish with the fingers, explains
the necessity for the basins and lavers, sometimes of silver, but usually of less costly
metals, which were served for the use of the

guests. Towels were provided and each person had his table napkin. Their use is indicated in a line of Gavin Douglas's *Æneid*, where he speaks of " soft serviettis to make their handis clene " ; and how this was done may be inferred from Welldon's description of James VI, who, he tells us, " rubbed his fingers' ends slightly with the wet end of a napkin." Wellbred persons of the time were counselled to avoid gluttony, to eat without suffocating themselves and not to stare rudely at others eating ; they were also to drink moderately, diluting their wine, and not to suck in their liquor " as if it were an egg "—meaning, I suppose, audibly —and finally they must not, while drinking, let their eyes roll about to this side and that.

Looking round the hall, we see that the floor is covered with rushes or bent grass. A " lyar," or rug, is stretched in front of the fire, and on it are several cushions serving as footstools. At the opposite end of the hall from the dais is a rude gallery in which two or three pipers or fiddlers are exercising their art, and in the corner of the hall below them are some stands of armour with spears and staves, while a " blawin' horn " hangs on the wall. There is also on one side of the hall a kind of service table, not a board detachable from its supports, but a solid table, such as was called in England a " table dormant." On this any vessels of silver or pewter that are not in use may be displayed. The only other piece of furniture is a chest, in which napery is kept and which serves also as a seat. In the shadow of a deep window we may perhaps discover a spinning-wheel, and beside it, on a cushion on the stone seat, a " buke of storeis," its parchment leaves enclosed in boards clasped with silver. On the wall by the fire-place the light of the flickering candles finds answering points of reflection in the gilding of a polychrome figure in carved wood, representing some favourite saint, St. Ninian, perhaps, or St. Kentigern.

Now the first thing that strikes us in this picture of the hall is how little furniture it contains. Tables and forms, with a chair for the master of the house, a side table and a chest, these are all that we find in a large room where all that is important in the social life of the house takes place. Why is the hall so scantily furnished ? We know that pieces of furniture of many types were in use—" copamries," " covartur-amries," " meit-amries," " vessel-almeries," " wair-almries " and " wairstalls," besides chests and coffers of various kinds. Yet these seldom appeared in the hall. Furniture in Scotland was made for convenience, not for display, to keep dishes and napery out of the way of dust and accidents, and it was accordingly made locally of fir or other cheap wood, and consisted of plain, serviceable pieces with little or no pretension to artistic treatment. On the other hand, the foreign furniture which was being imported by Halyburton and others had hardly begun to reach the private houses. The Church, by virtue of her wealth and her foreign connections, was still the pioneer in introducing the luxuries of civilisation, and it is to ecclesiastics that Halyburton sends most of the tapestries and furniture that appear in his Ledger. It is early in the sixteenth century before we find much Flemish or French furniture in the houses of the laity. Yet we do find references, exceptional rather than typical, to the " lang-sadyll " or settle, the " lettron " or reading desk, and to Flanderis kists and counters, pieces of furniture such as Halyburton was importing. Goods of foreign origin which were much more widely diffused were silver salt-fatts and other vessels, brazen chandillars and candlesticks, feather-beds, pillows and cushions, and, of course, napery. One entry in Halyburton's Ledger may be specially mentioned—a reference to an " oralag " sent by Bishop Elphinston for repair, and returned " mended, and the cais new." This shows that clocks were already in use in Scotland for ecclesiastical and public buildings, if not yet for domestic purposes.

Let us examine in rather more detail some of the furnishings and arrangements of the hall. The dining tables were merely long boards, of oak or fir, supported by a pair of trestles which were generally of fir, and when not in use the board was laid against the wall and the trestles were cleared away. There was no feeling that the room looked " unfurnished " without its tables. In the *Freiris of Berwik* we read how a " hostillar's " wife entertains a friar in her husband's absence. When the husband unexpectedly returns, she orders her maiden, according to Sibbald's version (1802), which professes to take no liberties with the text, to " clear the board." But if we turn to the Bannatyne MS., we find it is " *Close* yon board," a much more characteristic touch, implying that the table itself is to be dismounted and removed.

Go, clois yon burd, and tak awa the chyre
And lok up all into yone almery,
Baith met and drink with wyne and aill put by.

The reference to the single chair, which was the rightful seat of the master of the house, and to the use of the almery, are worth noting. We also read, earlier in the poem, that

The burde scho cuverit with clath of costly greyne,
Hir napry aboif wes woundir weill besene,

and early inventories show that table covers were, like the cloth of a modern billiard table, always green, a special cloth known as " Inglis green " being imported from England for the purpose.

The principal table, or " hie burde," set on the dais and having behind it the tapestry or other wall-hanging, was, as I have said, reserved for persons of importance, and the dais thus gave a line of social distinction. The author of *Schir Penny*, satirising the deference paid to wealth, in the person of Sir Penny, says :

> " That Syre is set on heich deiss
> And servit with mony rich meiss
> At the hie burde."

Some years ago a paper was read before a learned Society giving an account of an interesting sixteenth century inventory. The author, an experienced archæologist, had little knowledge of the social uses of the time, and the result was an extraordinary series of blunders. The first thing mentioned in the hall was " ane desbuyrd," meaning of course the table on the dais, and this was interpreted as " a dish-board, or perhaps a plate-rack." The author then pointed out the remarkable absence of chairs, mentioning that only one was specified, and that it stood in the hall, which, he said, " indicates a meagreness of plenishing not easily reconcilable even with the plain living of the times." The single chair, placed in the hall for the master's use, was the invariable rule at the period of which he wrote, and chairs did not come into ordinary domestic use till the seventeenth century. The author of the paper also interpreted " treying copes " as trying cups, which he thought might mean measuring cups, whereas they are simply " tree-en " cups, or cups made of wood ; and a " wairstall," a kind of press, he converted into a night stool, a brilliant effort of fancy ! Most of these mistakes arise not merely from ignorance of the terminology of house furniture of the time, but from failing to realise the difference between the domestic arrangements and social life of that age and those of our own day. Early furniture owes much of its interest to its reflecting customs with which we are no longer familiar, and it is meaningless unless we interpret it in terms of the social habits which produced it.

In Henryson's poem, *The Twa Mice*, we read how the cat catches one of the mice, and how, in playing with her victim :

Quhyll wad she let her ryn under the strae

—the straw with which the floor was covered. The mouse manages to escape, and Sibbald's version (1802) tells us that she crept " between the dressour and the wall " and climbed " behind the panelling." Now the words " dressour " and " panelling " were not in use in Scotland when the poem was written, and their introduction is but another instance of the propensity to substitute for unfamiliar expressions others more easily understood and perhaps considered more picturesque. When we consult the early text we find that the mouse escapes, not between the dressour and the wall, but between " ane burde and the wall," and climbs, not behind the panelling, but behind " ane parelling," which was the usual name for the hanging on the wall behind the dais table. The burde, taken from its trestles, had no doubt been laid along the foot of the wall, and the mouse, getting behind it, crept beneath the parelling and worked her way into a position of safety. Accordingly she says, later in the poem :

> I thank yone courtyne and yone perpall wall
> For my defence now fra ane crewel beist,

the perpall wall being the partition wall on which the courtyne or parelling hung.

A very interesting and characteristic piece of furniture in the Scottish mediæval hall was the Comptour, or Counter. Few houses in the fifteenth and sixteenth centuries were without one, yet to-day there are the most conflicting ideas as to what the counter really was, and what part it played in the domestic life of the time. It has been defined as a table, a cabinet, a desk and so on, while one reference in an old protocol book has been held to prove that it was a penannular, or C-shaped, sofa. Let us see what we can learn from documents of the time when the counter was in everyday use. But we must bear in mind that in any investigation into early furniture and its nomenclature we are dealing with names which, though stereotyped themselves, are applied to furniture forms which are constantly being modified and transformed in the attempt to adapt them to the varying uses of a rapidly developing social system. Especially is this true of pieces of furniture whose use is not limited by having to meet some definite and permanent human need. Beds, dining-tables and chairs, for example, are controlled by a certain fixed basis of human requirement ; and, under all their superficial varieties of form, their essential shape and measurements must have a certain relation to the scale and movements of the human figure. But when furniture is not so closely bound by elementary needs, the form remains comparatively indeterminate, and may vary in any direction according to the wants of those for whom it is made. Thus a name may persist long after it has ceased to be a correct description of the thing. A Cupboard, for instance—originally a table for displaying cups —has so changed its use and form that it has now nothing to do with cups, it is not a table, and it is used rather for concealment than display. A Gardevyand, originally intended, as its name implies, for storing food, developed into a sort of portable strong box, so that we read of locks and " braycis " being added to the King's " cardiviance " in order to " twrss west " the gold and silver vessels of James IV " again Yule to Lythgow." In the same way we read of a " meit-almery for conserving napery " and a " capamre " (or cup-almrie) for holding clothes. Thus the name of a piece of furniture must not be taken as indicating anything more than its original use.

The counter, compter-buird or compt burde, was originally a table whose top was used as a reckoning board, being marked out into spaces with distinguishing symbols. It was used for such purposes as adding up accounts, and for these calculations disc-shaped counters or jettons were employed. When not in use the jettons were kept in metal cylindrical cases, referred to in Halyburton's Ledger as " nests of countaris." A reference to the use of the compter burde for calculating occurs in Calderwood's *History of the Kirk of Scotland*, where we are told, as one incident of an earthquake in 1597, that " a man in St. Johnston, laying compts with his compters, the compts lap off the buird ; the man's thighs trembled, and," adds the faithful historian, " ane leg went up and the other doun." Counter boards were tables of convenient size and they were built on fixed legs, not simply laid on trestles. When we bear in mind that these tables, which were originally imported from Flanders, were the only tables known except the cumbrous long boards and trestles used for meals, we need not be surprised that they soon came into common use even among those who had little need for arithmetical calculation, but who appreciated the usefulness of a steady, moderate-sized table for many domestic purposes. Early inven tories show that in a large number of houses there was no table but the counter ; sometimes " ane comptar with the furmes " is mentioned, clearly showing that it was used for the house- hold meals. Mediæval illustration proves that the reckoning board was sometimes provided on the table-cloth, and this would enable the table itself to be without special marking and so to lose its arithmetical associations.

There is documentary evidence that as the counter developed as a piece of furniture it was made with some enclosed accommodation below. Thus Sir David Lyndsay, of the Mount, left among his furnishings " ane lokit comptar burde," and we find in the second half of the sixteenth century an increasing number of references to the locks and keys of counters, implying that they had closed receptacles. As time went on the enclosed accommodation seems to have extended downwards till it bccame the characteristic feature of the counter, and what had been the surface of the table now shrank in importance till it was merely the top of a small rectangular almeric. In the seventeenth century we read of " counter-almries " ; and in the list issued in 1612 of foreign goods subject to duty on import to Scotland, we find a fixed rate levied on " cabinettis or countaris." Thus the counter, which, under the name of " ane stop-compter," had been used for the display of stoups or vessels as early as 1489, had gone through a similar course of development to that of the cupboard in England. The counter, as an article of domestic furniture, seems to have gone out of use, or at least to have been superseded by other forms of table and cupboard, about the middle of the seventeenth century. It was retained, however, among merchants and tradesmen as a useful piece of business furniture, and the shop and bank counters of our day are thus survivals or developments of a forgotten mediæval form.

In connection with the vessels which stood upon the counter when it was used as a side table, one interesting question arises. What is meant by the " compterfute weschel " which often appears in early lists of household goods ?

In an English inventory of 1487, quoted as an appendix to the Paston Letters, we read of " ij garnysshe " (i.e. two complete sets) " of pewter vessel counterfete " ; and, according to an inventory of 1598, transcribed in the *Black Book of Taymouth*, there were " off counterfute plaittis in the galarie garderob of Balloch, iiij dosane " These are the only references I have found to counterfute dishes in the plural, and in these cases it is probable that a counterfeit metal is intended, though it is hard to say what is meant by pewter counterfeit. The dictionaries interpret " compterfute " in the sense of " imitation," an inferior metal meant to imitate one more valuable, and they give no alternative definition. As a matter of fact the base metal made to resemble gold was commonly called " alchemy."

But the references in early Scottish inventories are nearly always to " ane compterfute vessel," or simply " ane comptarfut," in the singular, and when this is mentioned as one particular vessel among others whose character or use is stated, it is difficult to resist the conclusion that the name was applied to a vessel serving a specific purpose or occupying a particular place. This impression is confirmed when we find the counterfoot grouped with vessels which were certainly silver ; and any lingering uncertainty disappears when we read, in a carefully detailed inventory of 1542, of a counterfoot expressly stated to be of silver, its weight being given and worked out at the value of silver per ounce. What a " comptarfut " was must remain a matter of conjecture till some literary reference is found which throws light on the problem. The word might conceivably be applied to a vessel cast in two halves ; or, as an alternative suggestion, it might be used of a vessel which stood at the foot of, or underneath, the counter—perhaps on a tray contained between the stretchers near the ground, just as we see vessels displayed in this position in early illustrations of similar pieces of furniture in other countries, such as credences and dressers.

Let us pass from the Hall to another room which is often mentioned in documents as to old Scottish houses, the " Chalmer of Des." The name has, like other mediæval terms, dropped out of use ; I do not think it is mentioned in McGibbon and Ross, and its meaning has puzzled antiquarians and lexicographers. Jamieson, discussing the corruption " chambradeeze," properly dismisses the suggestion that it stood for " la chambre où ils disent," and tells us that the word was still in use among old people in Fife for a parlour, and that the original form was " Chamber of Dais." Sir

Walter Scott said it was still common in his day
in the South of Scotland, and was applied to
the best sleeping room ; and he suggested that
it was the room in which there was a bed with
a dais, or canopy. But the term originated in
castles where there were many beds with
canopies, but only one Chamber of Dais ;
and, moreover, in Scottish records the word dais
is applied to the raised platform, and not, as in
France, to the canopy, which is called the
" cannabie " or " rufe," or sometimes, in connection with beds, the " sparwort." A study
of early inventories leaves little doubt that the
Chamber of Dais was the private apartment
which so often communicated with the upper
or dais end of the hall. It was the bedchamber
of the master of the house, and it was also used,
in accordance with mediæval custom, as a
retiring room for those who sat at the dais table.
Those who sat there represented what is called
" the quality," and the chamber was for their
exclusive use. Its position and use are clearly
shown by an extract from an old protocol book,
which tells us that Peter Rankin, the heir of
Shield, " entered the hall of Scheld and the
chalmer of des within the hall " (meaning that
to reach it he had to go through the hall). After
describing the furniture which he found in the
hall it goes on, " and in the chalmer of des he
found twa fedder beddis with necessaries, and

a wooden press." It is evident that the Chamber of Dais was in effect the principal bedroom.

I have spoken of the bareness of the hall in the matter of furniture, but the furnishing of the bedrooms was equally meagre, and this simply because of the primitive standard of comfort of the times. Even in an English house so richly furnished as Arundel Castle, the furnishing of the King's Chamber, so late as the year 1580, consisted only of a bed, a table and a chair, besides the tapestry hangings. We need not expect to find a more luxurious standard in Scotland. In the well-equipped house of Lord Lindsay of Byres—a house which had its own private chapel with suitable vestments and a gilded chalice—the Chalmer of Des had no furniture but the bed and " an ald compter," on which stood a candle and two books. In nearly all the other bedrooms of the house there was nothing but the bed or beds, for it was common to put several beds in one room. Occasionally there is a chest to hold clothes, or a form or stool, but nothing else was considered necessary. The bed, however, was often fitted with a " futegang," corresponding to the French " *marchepied* "—the long step or stool which we see in mediæval illustrations placed along the side of the bed. The " futegang " was sometimes " bandit," that is, hinged, so that the top could be opened and the inside used for keeping clothes, and in this form it is sometimes called a " buncar."

We need not concern ourselves with kitchen furniture nor with the equipment of the brew-house and bakehouse which were found in every mediæval mansion. If what has been said conveys the impression that life in a Scottish mediæval castle must have been a stern and comfortless existence, remember that a hardy race is not reared in luxury. Cast your minds back to the Scotland of that day, set far from the centres of mediæval culture, hard pressed to hold her own against her richer and more powerful neighbour ; a land of mountain and moor, shrouded with mist, drenched with rain, visited with short and fitful summers and long and bitter winters, and predestined to a history of jealous factions and relentless feuds ; and remember that in this land was reared a race hard-headed, resolute and tenacious, yet ever quick to shed its blood for a great cause, a dear name or a fine point of doctrine ; a race ready to go forth to other lands, however distant and however inhospitable, in quest of profit or adventure ; yet with hearts that kept turning always homeward with something of the passion which a man cherishes for the mother who has borne him in pain and nurtured him in poverty.

THE WEALTH OF THE CHURCH: A PRE-REFORMATION MANSE

THE SIXTEENTH CENTURY

The wealth of the Church as a factor in the Reformation movement—Relation of the movement to the Renaissance—Humanism within the Church—The Parson of Stobo; his revenues, etc.—The manse in Glasgow and its inmates—A disappointed nephew—The parson's bedchamber—Rich hangings and furniture—An unexpected apparition—Coffers and chests and their contents—Early regulations as to clerical costume—The parson's costly apparel—" The oratour within his hous "—The altar and its furnishings—Vestments—Sacred and secular books—The hall—Carved furniture—Cupboard of plate—Significance of plate in mediæval times—The kitchen—" Large tabling and belly cheer "—Stores of provisions and fuel—Riding kit and armour—Sport and recreations—Tame animals—An early chiming clock—The parson's death—The people and the Church.

WHATEVER line of interest may lead one to the study of Scotland in the sixteenth century, one cannot go far without becoming conscious of a deep and irresistible current surging through the national life of the time. Everywhere there is transition, progress, change. Whatever new facts research may reveal, in this department or in that, the interest of these as isolated facts soon gives place to a sense of their significance as reflecting the general movement of the age. So it is with the study of domestic furnishing. As we review the documentary records of house plenishings in the sixteenth century we are brought face to face with two symptoms of the time too conspicuous to be passed by. The first of these is the wealth of the Church, a material prosperity strikingly disproportionate to the general economic condition of the country. The second is the appearance of the middle class, and its rapid advance in wealth and social importance. These two phenomena cannot strictly be separated, or treated as if they had no relation to each other. As a matter of fact the Church lost her economic leadership just because civilisation became gradually too complex for her control, and because the trades and crafts which had grown up under her patronage became so highly specialised as to call for skilled and trained men to conduct and manage them ; and with her economic leadership the Church lost, of course, a large part of her hold on the people. And, on the other hand, the revolt against the corruptions and exactions of the Church proved a powerful factor in educating the people, in developing their capacity for independent judgment, and in fitting them for the political influence which they were destined to exercise. Still, it will be convenient to treat these two

distinctive features of the life of the time
separately, and in the present lecture we shall
limit ourselves to the wealth of the Church as
one of the elements which led up to the Reformation. With the ecclesiastical controversies
of the time we need not concern ourselves.
Even the historical results of the Reformation—
the abolition of the papal power in Scotland and
the establishment of the reformed religion—
interest us here only in some of their consequences. But the Reformation movement has
this signal importance for us, that it was the
crisis in which the modern spirit sought for a
decisive victory in its conflict with mediæval-
ism ; and that it provided Scotland with a sharp
issue on which every man was able to take a side,
and so helped to bring the country to a knowledge of its own character and its own destiny.

Let us beware, however, of thinking of the
Reformation as a local movement, the product
of merely local conditions. Both the decay
within the Church, and the spirit of criticism
and revolt without, were largely due to the
breaking up of old standards of thought and of
conduct, and to the emancipation from accustomed restraints, which followed, all over
Europe, from the Renaissance. In every
country, and in every department of life, sub-
mission to authority gave place to the exercise
of individual judgment. Long acknowledged

codes were challenged, and as their control weakened there was an inevitable tendency to revert to an undisciplined paganism.

Within the borders of the Church itself these changes soon began to bear bitter fruit. In the intoxicating atmosphere of humanism spirituality began to wither and to lose its vital and inspiring force. The beauty of holiness and the rapture of self-consecration were fading visions that seemed more and more spectral and delusive. The call of the old austere ideals of poverty and self-mortification now sounded faint and far away—the dying echo of a crazy enthusiasm. While there were many in the Church who, like Bishop Elphinstone in Scotland, upheld the highest traditions of their office, there were many more who preferred to work out their careers as ambitious nobles and scheming men of the world. In an age when every institution, however venerable, was subjected to searching criticism, it was inevitable that the revolt against a degenerate Church, whose sway had been absolute and was now felt oppressive, should everywhere be a characteristic consequence of the Renaissance. Elsewhere, however, that conflict might be subsidiary to other manifestations of the new spirit—to a vigorous outburst of artistic or literary activity, or to an effort for constitutional liberty. In Scotland it was the problem on which all the national energies were brought to a focus. There the ecclesiastical abuses were not less flagrant than elsewhere ; and there the opulence of the Church was thrown into sharp relief against the poverty of the people.

Catholic writers, while admitting that there was much that was reprehensible in the lives of the clergy, maintain that the attack on the Church was largely inspired by the cupidity of the nobles, who had remained impoverished since the War of Independence ; and it cannot be disputed that there is much historical evidence of the existence of such sordid motives. But from this point of view, no less than from the opposite one, the wealth of the Church is admitted to be an element of crucial importance in accounting for the course of Scottish history in the sixteenth century. It is said that practically half the wealth of the country was in the hands of the Church. We have already seen how most of the rich furnishings and luxuries sent into Scotland by Andrew Halyburton were consigned to ecclesiastics. And Cardinal Beatoun, we are told, kept such a house " as was never holden in Scotland under a King." But general statements and exceptional instances do not give us a picture of the wealth of the Church as it struck the eye of contemporary observers. Little or nothing has been written as to the actual conditions of the home life of the ordinary clergy. To fill this gap and to give you a glimpse of the interior of a Pre-Reformation manse and its furnishings, I propose to describe the home of a Scottish priest who drew his revenues from a thinly populated district in Tweedside and who was one of the Canons of Glasgow Cathedral.

In February of the year 1542 there died, at his house in Glasgow, Maister Adam Colquhoun, " persone of Stobo." The manse of Stobo stood at the head of the Drygate of Glasgow, and was one of the many houses in that quarter occupied by the Cathedral clergy. The Chapter of Glasgow consisted of thirty-two canonries or prebends, and of these the canonry of Stobo was not the least desirable. The benefice of Stobo brought in an income of two thousand merks a year, and that of Broughton, which went with it, another thousand merks, representing in all two thousand pounds of the money of the realm at that date. Jóhn Major, writing of Glasgow in Colquhoun's time, says, " the Church possesses prebends many and fat ; but in Scotland such revenues are enjoyed *in absentia* just as they would be *in presentia*," a custom which he deplores. The cure of souls in Stobo was in the hands of a rural vicar, John Colquhoun, probably a relative of Maister Adam. It was expected of the prebendary, however, that he should pay periodical visits in order to superintend his rural charge. During such absences he was represented in the Chapter by a Vicar of Stalls, to whom he had to make an annual payment of twelve merks a year, along with a cope and surplice. There was also an ordinance, dating from 1401, which " considering the great and detestable deficiency of the ornaments " from which the Cathedral had suffered in its divine services, levied a tax on the various prebendaries for copes, chasubles, dalmatics, tunics and other ornaments. For this purpose the Parson of Stobo had to contribute five pounds. These, however, with perhaps a small salary to his vicar, seem to have been the only charges against his income.

As to Maister Adam Colquhoun himself, he was a younger son of Patrick Colquhoun of Glens, who owned property in the Stable Green at the western end of the Cathedral. A few scattered references to him in early records suggest that he may have been somewhat high-handed and given to contention. The Glasgow Diocesan Registers record a dispute between him, when as a younger man he was Rector of Biggar, and the neighbouring Rector of Skirling on a question of tithes ; and after he had been promoted to be Rector of Govan, a Glasgow canonry, he was charged with taking possession of part of the Rector of Renfrew's manse during his absence. One other fact may be mentioned which has some interest. He inherited a house in Stable Green which he sold to Matthew Stewart, second Earl of Lennox, and it was in this house that Darnley, years afterwards, lay sick on the memorable occasion when Queen Mary visited him and " taried certen daies withe him " two or three weeks before his murder.

The manse of Stobo, whose furnishings we are to describe, is said to have been a tall, tower-like house, very solidly built of stone. It was entered by a winding stone stair in an outside tower pierced by narrow slits which admitted but little light, and the doors of the apartments, as was usual at that time, opened direct from the stair, or from other rooms, there being no passages. There were spacious fireplaces with carved lintels in the hall and in the parson's own chamber, and near the fireplaces there were little aumries let into the walls. The interiors were gloomy and prison-like, for the light entered by small windows through walls which were three feet thick. At the back of the house, facing south, there were wooden galleries which pleasantly overlooked the garden and orchard running down to the burn, and enabled the occupants to take advantage of such sunlight and fresh air as the climate and season afforded.

When his last " seiknes " was upon him, the household included, besides the dying man, his two natural sons, James and Adam, and their mother, Jane Boyd, who no doubt tended him in his hour of extremity. But there was also living a nephew, Peter Colquhoun, described as " a citinar of Glasgow," who, after his uncle's death, claimed to be the legal heir. This nephew charged the two natural sons and their mother, along with James Houston, sub-dean of Glasgow, and Master Archibald Crau-furd, parson of Eaglesham, whose manse was next door, with " wrangously intromitting " with the goods of the late Master Adam during his illness and after his death ; and moved the Lords of Council to cause the defenders to deliver up the " gudis of airschip or the avail thereof " as " now pertening to the said Peter be resoun of airschip throw deceis of his umquhile eme "—or late uncle. What were the pleas advanced by the parties to this law-suit, we are not told. But if Peter was trusting to the sons of a celibate priest having no legal status he was leaning on a broken reed. For in the Register of the Privy Seal we find that on 5 February, 1529–30, James and Ade Colquhoun, sons of Mr. Ade Colquhoun, Parson of Stobo, had been formally legitimated. The Lords of Council accordingly assoilzied the defendants, and the unfortunate Peter lost his

case. His claim, however, gives so full a descrip
tion of his uncle's possessions that we can form a
tolerably clear picture of what must have been
a remarkable house.

Let us begin with the parson's own chamber.
Here there was a bed of richly carved wood
decorated with gold, in which Master Adam
slept soft o' nights on a feather mattress containing 140 lb. of down—nearly double the
quantity that is put into the best modern
feather bed. His head, dressed with " nycht
hair-gear " and covered with a " nycht courche,"
rested on luxurious down pillows " warit," or
covered, with holland cloth. The sheets were
of the same fine material, and for warmth in
the raw Glasgow nights there were first a pair
of " pladdis," and over these a pair of blankets
of fine fustian. Draughts were kept off by a
pair of damask curtains " of divers hewis,
fassit with silk and knoppit (or tasselled) with
gold." By day a pair of head-sheets was laid
across the pillows, a covering of rich velvet
lined with fustian was stretched over the bed,
while above this was spread a blue mantle.

When morning came, and the priest, awaking
in his carved and gilded bed, cast his eyes
around him, he had reason to be satisfied with
the beauty and luxury of his surroundings, all
the more so when we remember how scantily
the bedrooms of the time were usually furnished.

Round the walls hung panels of arras work—
some perhaps of the charming " *verdure* " of
mediæval times, designed with foliage and
flowers, and varied, as was customary, with
little animals such as squirrels and monkeys,
or rabbits disappearing into their burrows ; and
others with " portraiture of huntsman, hawk
and hound," or scenes from some scriptural
story or secular romance. We read of there
being twelve of these panels in the chamber, but
probably some of these had been removed from
the hall. Against this tapestried background of
harmonious, low-toned colour—low toned not
from age but from the subdued illumination—
appeared a large brazen chandillar, hung from
the ceiling, with its tall white candles. In
front of the fireplace stood a " langsadill bed of
carvit werk "—an oak settle on which the priest
may have sat musing by the fire the night
before. In a corner of the room was a press,
also of carved oak, with a curtain of damask
hanging before it to protect the costly raiment
that lay within. A carved chest stood at the
foot of the bed. It was the practice to keep
valuables in the bedroom, where the owner
could keep watch over them, and they were
stored in chests and boxes of various kinds for
convenience of removal in case of fire or other
alarm. Master Adam Colquhoun, having a
large quantity of valuables, required a good

many receptacles for their security. Besides the carved chest there was a " shrine," which was simply another form of chest, having none of the sacred associations we attach to the word ; a " balhuise," the Scottish form of the French " *bahut*," meaning a box, or possibly in those days a hutch ; a coffer, a " gardyviat " or strong box, and a " maill of ledder lokkit," or in other words a locked leather trunk.

The " water-pot " is of silver. Standing perhaps on one of the larger chests, either by the bedside or under a window, there was a sponge, a rubber and a locked case of combs. The rubber was apparently a brush, as we read of hogs' bristles being used in the sixteenth century " for to make rubbers and brushes." These toilet accessories complete the furnishing of the bedroom, though we have still to examine the contents of the chests and of the clothes-press. But here the inventory supplies one of those delightful, because so unexpected, touches which suddenly give life to the pictures that come down to us of the long-forgotten past. Here, in his bed-chamber, it seems, the parson, with his taste for gay and bright-coloured things and for amusing companionship, keeps a parrot, which we may imagine perched on the back of the settle, cocking a speculative and judicious eye over the yawnings and stretchings of his newly awakened master. Even the clerk

who drafted the inventory seems to have felt
the abruptness of this apparition on his blame-
less page, and he discreetly and decorously
softens it by introducing it as " a bird, viz. a
parrok."

Let us look now at some of the precious
things contained in the coffers and chests.
There is a " pair of beidis "—that is, a set of
beads, or a rosary—" with v. gaudeis, ilk gaud
contenand ane double portingale ducat," the
whole being valued at sixty-three pounds. A
cross of gold, weighing 4 oz., is valued at
thirty-two pounds. These values are in Scots
money, which at that time was worth about a
fourth part of English money ; but if the cross
was pure gold, as it no doubt was, it would
represent a present-day value of sixteen guineas
for the metal alone, apart from workmanship
and other elements which might add to its
value. There is also a precious relic, a tablet
of gold hung with a small chain of 4 oz. in
weight, with " ane pece of the haly croce intill
it " ; and this is said to be worth " tua hun-
dretht pund." Most costly of all is a chain of
four hundred Crowns of the Sun, valued at
five hundred pounds ; but this perhaps is to
be regarded as merely a method of hoarding
money. Among smaller objects of value are
a signet of gold ; a gold ring with a fine " safer "
(sapphire) stone, worth one hundred pounds ;

a double Portugal ducat, worth twelve pounds ; and a " woup " or circlet of gold serving as an armlet, of 1 lb. weight, and representing a value of ninety-six pounds. In one of the boxes there is also carefully stowed away a " pair of punzeonis of claitht of gold, price x li."

Scots poetry of the time is full of embittered allusions to the faults and vices of the clergy. In the *Satyre of the Thrie Estaitis* their rapacity and their oppression of the poor is mercilessly exposed. Another satirical poem, after dealing with their immorality, their ostentatious luxury and their neglect of their charges, goes on to say

So mony preistis cled up in secular weid
With blasing breistis casting their claithis on breid,
　　It is no need to tell of quhome I mein,
So few to tell the dargey and the beid
　　Within this land was nevir hard nor sene.

—the " dargey " being the " Dirige," the Office of the Dead, at matins. However regular the Parson of Stobo may have been at his clerical duties, it must be confessed that he did not deny himself the pleasure of flaunting in " secular weid," and displaying what may fairly be called a " blasing breist " to all whom he encountered in the streets of Glasgow. But before passing judgment on his costume it is fair to remember that there was in those days no recognised clerical dress by which the wearers could be distinguished at a glance from laymen. A thirteenth-century statute ordains that the clergy shall not wear " red or striped clothes, nor clothes conspicuous for too great shortness "— a law which some have interpreted as being directed against the clerical use of tartan and the kilt ! Another statute, enacted only a few years after Colquhoun's death, forbade the use of " top-boots, double-breasted and oddly-cut coats, or coats of forbidden colours, as yellow, green and such kinds of parti-colour," and prescribed the wearing of cassocks for town use. From these and similar decrees we learn that while the Church enjoined a becoming gravity of costume on the clergy, both in regard to colour and material, there was, in fact, a constant tendency to disregard such counsels and to indulge personal vanity and caprice.

The Parson of Stobo's ordinary costume seems to have consisted of a doublet of crammesy velvet lined with scarlet, with a waistcoat or wilecoat, also of scarlet, worn over a shirt of white holland cloth. His hose are of Paris black and they are bound with gartans of silk with gold tassels at the side. A silken belt, also with gold tassels, encircles his waist, while at his hip hangs a bag of crammesy velvet with massive gold mountings. Wearing a pair of velvet shoes he crosses to the carved press in the corner of his chamber and draws aside the curtain, taking out a rich gown of damask lined with marten sable. This he throws round his shoulders and fastens in front with a button of wrought gold, matching a similar button on the breast of his doublet. To complete his toilet he puts on a " litel bonet of welvot sewit with gold," tucks a pair of cloth gloves " pirnit " or interwoven with gold into his belt ; and then, fastening on his " quhinger," which is ourgilt with gold, and slipping his silver toothpick into the bag at his waist, he is ready for the day's duties and adventures.

What there is of ecclesiastical costume, or vestments, is kept not in the bedchamber but partly in some small room or press near the kitchen on the ground-floor ; so that in passing out to the Cathedral he could conveniently lay his hands upon whatever might be required. There was " ane round preistis bonet "—the biretta which was prescribed as conforming with " the ancient custom of the clergy," and which they had to be enjoined to remove in church, " especially in time of divine service." Three surplaits, or surplices, are mentioned : one of crape, one of lawn and one of holland. Also a " hude of crammase satyn with welvot, drawin with ane string of gold, price xx li " ; an " almos," or almuce (*L. almucia*), valued at xl li. and another cape " firrit with spottit arming " (ermine) valued at x li.

It is difficult to arrive at a fair estimate of the costliness of the sumptuous apparel that has been described. No mere conversion of Scots money into sterling is of much use as a basis for a comparison with present-day expenditure, for the modern use of machinery in manufactures, and modern facilities of intercourse with foreign countries and many other causes, have accustomed us to a scale of relative values that is very unlike that of mediæval times. We know from Halyburton's Ledger, for example, that velvet costs ten or twelve times as much as Arras tapestry of the quality usually imported into Scotland. It seems surprising, too, to us that a mantle or gown whose materials cost perhaps from sixty to a hundred pounds, should not have exceeded five shillings for the making. Such facts, while easily enough explained, illustrate the difficulty of comparing mediæval and modern expenditure. However, it is enough to note the Parson of Stobo's preference for velvet, the most costly of all the ordinary materials in use, and especially for crimson velvet, which was more expensive than other colours ; and how his gown is lined with marten sable, the most expensive of furs ; and how almost everything he wears is ornamented with gold, so that even the bag that hangs at his waist has " irnes," or mountings, that would melt down into thirty-three of our present-day sovereigns. However picturesque, to our modern eyes, may be the splendidly arrayed figure of the Parson of Stobo, his costume shows little sympathy with the ideal of an ascetic frugality, nor can it be said to exemplify that sobriety of colour and material which was prescribed by the authority of the Church.

Leaving the bedchamber we enter a small but extremely interesting room, described as " the oratour within his bous." Its principal feature is, of course, the altar, placed against the eastern wall and hung with a frontal of black velvet with fringes of gold. It has two coverings of fine holland cloth. On the top of the altar rests the " altar stane " or super-altar, the small consecrated slab which was laid on the middle of an altar not itself conse-crated. Persons of importance were sometimes granted the privilege of having one of these consecrated altar stones to carry with them while travelling, so that they could have a mass said by their chaplains even if there were no fixed consecrated altar of which use could be made. On the altar stood the sacred vessels— " ane chalice and patene of silver ourgilt with gold," and, on a silver plate, two silver " crowat-tis," or cruets, containing respectively the wine and the water for the Eucharist. The plate served the purpose of catching any drip from the cruets. There was also—what was very

unusual except in richly furnished churches—
a silver spoon, used to measure out the small
quantity of water mixed with the wine in pre-
paring the chalice ; and employed also for
removing flies or the like from the chalice. A
silver sacring bell, which was rung at the conse-
cration, also stood on the altar. And, finally,
there was a cushion made of cloth of silver, on
which was laid a " mess buke," or missal, of
parchment, its pages penned by hand in black
and red Gothic lettering and richly illuminated
in colours and gold.

At each end of the altar a rod projected from
the wall and supported a damask curtain which
hung close to, and in a plane parallel to, the end
of the altar.

In the oratory too were kept the vestments ;
a chasuble which, like the altar frontal, was of
black velvet ; a stole and a " fannale " (fannon)
or maniple, both made of velvet, the maniple
being worn on the priest's left wrist ; an
" amyt," or amice, which was a linen hood
lowered so as to encircle the neck ; and a belt,
probably made to match the vestments and
taking the place of the more usual girdle of
white cord.

The only piece of furniture in the oratory
that remains to be mentioned was a carved desk
or prie-dieu. On its top lay a large velvet
cushion on which rested the priest's " orasoun

buke, coverit with grene velvet." This was no doubt an illuminated *Book of Hours*, containing the abridged choir services in honour of the Virgin, consisting of psalms, lessons from scripture and anthems. The desk was probably made with a side opening to a sort of aumrie with a shelf. Here, in a double row, were arranged the parson's " librell bukis," as they are called to distinguish them from the purely devotional books which have already been mentioned. They are secular books designed to cultivate the mind, providing what we still call a " liberal education." Among these volumes are " tua cours of the law, with utheris doctouris thair-upone," and evidence still survives that the Parson of Stobo had taken advantage of his opportunities and was looked upon as a man well versed in the law. There are also works on " theologie and vther science." In the prologue to Sir David Lindsay's contemporary poem, *The Tragedie of the Cardinal*, he tells us how

> Not lang ago, eftir the hour of prime,
>   Secreitlie sitting in my oratorie,
> I tuke ane buke till occupy the time,
>   Qubair I fand monie tragedie and storie
>   Quhilk Johne Boccas had put in memory,

and we may infer that it was usual to keep books in the oratory and to make use of it as a quiet study for secular as well as religious reading.

Passing to the Hall, we find a dignified apartment whose walls are hung with some of the panels of tapestry that were mentioned as being found in the bed-chamber. The wide fireplace, under its carved stone lintel, is fitted with a "chimnay" or grate, of iron. The furnishing is in accordance with the usual mediæval scheme, yet it illustrates too the advance towards a higher standard both of comfort and of conscious artistic interest. The meit-burde, with its trestles and forms, stands at one end of the room and is spread with the usual "coveringis and claithis thereof." Against the wall on one side stands a "cop burde of eistland burde carvit werk, quhair the silver weschel stude." The cupboard, as a piece of domestic furniture, was well known in England in the fourteenth century, but this is perhaps the first mention of its use in a private house in Scotland. It was fitted with shelves and arranged so that the contents were displayed when the doors were thrown open. In Scotland a counter or side table was all that was wanted in most private houses, as there was no profusion of silver vessels requiring special arrangements for their display. While the Parson of Stobo's silver was of such quantity and value as to call for a cupboard, it is interesting to find that his hall also contains a double counter of Flemish origin. It was no doubt used as a buffet or

service table, and this is confirmed by the fact
that the luxurious owner had provided " ii
coveringis, i to the counter i other to the burde
of the hall, maid of cusching werk." These
were no doubt of Flemish quilted work, and
they are an unusual luxury, costing about fourteen pounds for the two. Of the pieces of furniture mentioned the counter was evidently the
most important, as it is valued at twenty pounds,
whereas the cupboard only reaches half that sum,
and the hall table, along with its forms and
trestles, is put at less than three pounds. The
other furniture consisted of a " meit almery for
conserving of napry, silit abone," or having a
panelled top ; a settle, a chair and a " buffat
stule," all described as of carved work. Up-
holstered seats were of course as yet unknown,
but the hall was provided with " i dosane of fyne
grete cuschingis of Flanderis werk " for use on
the settle and other seats, as well as for footstools. They were stuffed with feathers
and were probably covered with *verdure*
tapestry.

But perhaps the most interesting feature of
the furnishing of the hall is the silver plate
which stood on the cupboard. Such a display
was of course characteristic of mediæval times,
though it is rather exceptional in early Scottish
records. There was little accumulated wealth
in Scotland ; her exports did not pay for her

imports, and there was also a constant drain of money due to other causes.

> I dar weill say, within this fiftie yeir
> Rome has ressavit furth of this regioun
> For bullis and benefice quhilk they buy full deir
> Quhilk micht full weill have payit ane kingis ransoum.
> Preistis suld na moir our substance sa consoum
> Sending yeirly sa greit riches to Rome.

Still, as Scotland gradually gained in wealth, and as more settled conditions gave the possessors of valuables some guarantee of security, it became usual for the well-to-do in Scotland, as elsewhere, to " garnish their cupboards with plate " ; so that a Scottish poet, calling on his countrymen to celebrate the destruction of the Spanish Armada, said :

> Expose your gold and shyning silver bright
> On covered cop-buirdes set in opin sight ;
> Ouer-gilted coups, with carved covers clear,
> Fine precious stanes, quhair they may best appear ;
> Lavers in ranks, and silver baissings shine
> Saltfats outshorne, and glasses crystalline.

In Master Adam Colquhoun's day such displays were less common, and his cupboard must have been considered an imposing one. It consisted of about forty separate vessels and dishes, weighing in all something like 65 lbs. troy weight of silver. There were five flagons of graduated sizes, the largest containing half a gallon ; three stoups, the largest containing a quart ; and four silver " pieces " with their covers, the largest containing a pint. The most massive of these vessels weighed as much as 8 lb. each. There was also a set of silver trenchers, a silver basin and laver, a silver cup and a goblet, each with its cover ; a silver maser and its cover both doubly overgilt ; a set of two dozen silver spoons, weighing 2 oz. each ; a silver salt-fatt with cover of silver doubly overgilt ; a silver " gerdyn," here apparently meaning a retort-shaped bottle ; a chargeour, a plate and a " compterfute," all of silver, and two silver dishes, one described as a " braid " dish and the other as a " luggit " dish, meaning a dish with projecting handles at opposite sides. Besides all these there is a pair of silver chandillars and, last but not least interesting, " ane cais of carving knyfis, Flanderis making, doublie ourgilt." The set contains twelve small knives, three " mekle " knives and a fork. The use of such a set of table knives marks a considerable advance on the earlier practice, according to which each man used the knife he carried about with him. The mention of a fork has a special interest. Forks were not in general use in England before the middle of the seventeenth century, though they were sometimes used for fruit. Thus Piers Gaveston had three silver forks for eating pears, and an English will of 1463 bequeathes " my silver forke for grene gyngour." Though the fork in the manse of Stobo is cased along with knives intended for meat, the fact that there is but one, along with what we know of mediæval usage, suggests that it was not used for meat with the knives, but kept for fruit and sweetmeats.

A cupboard so well garnished with silver plate is apt to suggest to us a rather purse-proud love of display. Yet this is hardly fair, as it leaves out of account the conditions and habits of the time. Wherever there was a surplus of income over necessary expenditure there was, in varying degree, according to the amount of that surplus and to the taste and temperament of the individual, a tendency to the accumulation of plate and other valuables. It must be remembered that banking did not as yet exist in Scotland ; though we find in Halyburton's Ledger that even in the fifteenth century sums were sent from Scotland to the great banking houses of Antwerp. We read too of considerable sums being forwarded to Halyburton to trade with " for the behuf and profyt " of some of his correspondents in Scotland. But on the whole there was little opening for the investment of accumulated savings. To lend money at interest was still apt to expose the lender to the odium associated with the practice of usury, as well as to legal penalties. The alternatives were thus to hoard money or to expend it in plate or rich furnishings which bore agreeable and unmistakable witness to the prosperity of the owner. In Harrison's contemporary account of Elizabethan England we are told that towards the end of a lease a successful farmer might have six or seven years' rent lying by him, " besides a fair garnish of pewter on his cupboard, with so much more in odd vessel going about the house, three or four feather beds, so many coverlids and carpets of tapestry, a silver salt, a bowl for wine, if not a whole nest, and a dozen of spoons to furnish up the suit." Such agricultural prosperity was an outcome of the expansion of English trade under Elizabeth, and so rapid had been the advance towards luxury that there were men then living who remembered when they had " laid on straw pallets or rough mats covered only with a sheet, under coverlets made of dagswain, and a good round log under their heads instead of a bolster or a pillow." In Scotland there was no such sudden increase of prosperity. Wealth was in fewer hands, and chiefly, as we have seen, in the hands of the Church. Even among the nobles there was comparatively little silver to display, most of the vessels in domestic use being of pewter.

The Kitchen need not detain us long. There are but two pieces of furniture, one a " weschell almeric," which was probably a plainly made kitchen dish-press, and the other a " dressing-

burd "—in other words a table on which meat
and other articles of food were dressed. No
form or stool or other kind of seat is provided,
nor is there any other concession to comfort.
Everything gives way to the claims of cookery.
There are cauldrons, kettles, " mekle " pots and
" litel " pots, frying pans, goose pans, roasting
irons, fish " skummers," " mekle speits " and
" litel speits," stoups, pitchers and " piggis," besides the special paraphernalia of the bake-house
and brew-house. A " capon-cave " shows that
poultry were kept, and the supply of provisions
is on a scale that suggests that the household
was given to what a contemporary calls " large
tabling and belly cheer." There are, for
example, eight marts, or salted carcases, of
beef ; a pipe of salmon, containing eight dozen ;
a pipe of Loch Fyne herring ; an ark containing forty bolls of meal ; six stone of butter,
and a " kebboc " of cheese weighing 22 lb.
Such supplies must have relieved Master Adam
of any acute anxiety as to his daily bread, particularly as beneficed clergymen were enjoined to
fare frugally and temperately at table, and to
avoid delicacy and superfluity in meat and
drinks. His fuel was also secure, for there is a
mow (or heap) of coals containing as much as
eighty loads ; and his barn is well stored with
wheat, oats, " beir," peas and hay.

Even in the stable there is much that is

characteristic and suggestive. His riding saddle has a " curpale " or crupper of velvet ; and there is a green " horse-house," the trappings of cloth with which the horse was draped in mediæval times. In the stable he keeps his riding kit, consisting of a damask riding gown lined with black, a velvet hood lined with damask, and a black cloak faced with velvet. Here too we find his armour, a habergeon of mail, a pair of brigandines for back and front, a " pesane " or gorget of mail, splints for legs and arms, gloves of plate and also of mail, helmets and other headgear, and a two-handed sword. The clergy, it may be mentioned, were forbidden to bear arms, yet a fight between two chaplains armed with " hyngers " is recorded in the Ripon Chapter Acts (Surtees Society) in the year 1503, and there are other evidences that the prohibition was not literally observed. There is also a single-handed sword of a more elegant and decorative character. It is doubly overgilt with gold, has a scabbard of velvet, " crampet," or provided with guards, of silver ; and it is slung from a belt of figured velvet. To carry on more peaceful occasions there is a " ganging staf of bressale, tippit with silver at baith ends and in the middis," bressale being brazil-wood, from which the country of Brazil derived its name. We find too that the Parson was a devotee of sport. He has a rather dandified outfit for archery—a hand-bow, arrow-bag and "caver" (quiver) with arrows, "ane bras of ovir beñe tippit with silver," meaning, I suppose, an ivory arm-guard with silver mountings ; and a shooting glove "sewit with silk and knoppit with gold." Another form of sport seems to have interested him. Among the popular grievances referred to in the *Generall Satyre* is the prevalence of coursing, to the destruction of the crops :

> Sic coursing, evin and morn,
> Quhilk slayis the corn, and fruct that growis grene.

and we find that the Parson of Stobo has a set of "rais cuppillis of silver" with silk collars "spenlit" (spindled ?) with silver, which were no doubt used in coursing for releasing the dogs. He has also a silken dog-leash and a dog-collar studded with silver. Along with his taste for sport goes a love of animals, and we find that, besides the parrot indoors, he keeps outside a tame hind and a crane.

One other remarkable possession is to be found in the stable—a "streking knok with bellis efferand thairto." Clocks were seldom found in Scotland at this period unless in churches and other public buildings. How Master Adam came to own a chiming clock is hard to say, and why it should be kept in the stable, unless the bells "efferand thairto" were too loud to be tolerated in the house, and had to be so far removed that distance might soften their stridency and render them tuneful and mellow enough to please the epicurean fancy of the fastidious priest.

It is wellnigh four hundred years since, perhaps with these very bells sounding in his ears, Master Adam Colquhoun drew his last breath, and the stiffening body was left lying on the gilded bed, in the shadow of the damask curtains with their fringes of silk and tassels of gold. It is not for us to allot to him the fate either of Dives or of Lazarus. He probably left behind an amiable memory. His collection of " librell bukis " on the law, theology and " uther science " shows that he was not one of those whose ignorance and illiteracy disgraced the Church. If his relations with Jane Boyd cannot be justified, they were at any rate only too characteristic of the time ; he seems at least to have been constant to her, and if the laws of the Church had permitted, he would doubtless have been an exemplary husband. How far the manse of Stobo may be taken as representative of the homes of the Pre-Reformation clergy is a question which we have not enough evidence to decide ; but it is at least remarkable that it presents us with a far more opulent and luxurious picture than any contemporary nobleman's house of which a record has been preserved. We are glad to remember those of the clergy whose devotion and spirituality survived the corrupting and disintegrating tendencies of the time, and were proof against the relaxed standards of the age. But the ostentatious wealth and worldliness of the clergy are so constant a theme, not only in the works of the satirists and in the pages of impartial history, but also, as evils to be combated, in the Statutes of the Church itself, that they must be accepted as outstanding features of contemporary life. Can we wonder, then, if the people, groaning under the exactions of the clergy and confronted with their material standards and their flagrant immoralities, and already, behind locked doors, reading in their own homely tongue the un-worldly teaching of the Sermon on the Mount, began to form opinions of their own on the fit-ness of the Church as a vehicle and exponent of the teaching of Christ ?

THE RISE OF THE BURGHERS; A CLOTH MERCHANT'S HOUSE; AND SOME DECORATIVE ARTS

THE SIXTEENTH CENTURY—*Continued*

The three estates—Rising importance of the burgher class—Dwelling-house of a sixteenth-century cloth merchant—The hall—Armour—The bedchamber—Agricultural implements—The booth—" Ane hingand brod of oley cullouris "—Early interest in painting in Scotland—Pictures and painted cloths—The burgesses as art patrons and introducers of foreign products and ideas—The " keiking glass "—The alarm clock—Some items in the inventory of Sir David Lyndsay of the Mount—Wood-carving in Scotland—Domestic panelling—Linenfold and other patterns—Carved wood from Montrose—At Ethie Castle—From Threave Castle—Cardinal Beaton's panels at Balfour House—Embroidery in early times—Its development in the sixteenth century—Queen Mary's embroideries—" Story work "—Various examples—The Rehoboam set—The Earl of Morton's set—Probable date and origin.

" THE Scottis peple," says Bishop Leslie, writing towards the end of the sixteenth century, " is diuidet in thrie ordouris ; ane, of thame quhais pietic and hett studdie of religione had addicted themselves planelie to serue the Kirke ; the secunde, of thame quhais nobilitie and bienes of blude hes placed (them) in the secunde degrie of the commoune weil ; the thrid, of thame quhome the

63

tounes accnawleges among thame to be frank
and frie." In the political development of the
country each of these orders, or estates, exercised in turn a predominating influence. It was
the nobility whom the earlier Jameses had to
conciliate, and whose support had to be secured
when a national policy was to be carried out.
But so heavy were the losses sustained by the
nobility at Flodden that from that time the
balance of power passed into the hands of the
Church. This position of influence the Church
made use of to encourage James V in his
adhesion to the French Alliance and the Catholic religion. As time went on, however, the
popular revolt against the abuses and exactions
of the Church was reinforced by a growing
recognition of the fact that England, rather than
France, was designed by nature to be Scotland's
ally. The pressure of such great questions as
these on the minds of the people, and the
groping for practical methods of settling them,
helped to train and educate them for the influence and responsibilities to which they were
destined in turn to succeed when the Reformation deprived the Church of Rome of her
temporal power in Scotland. It was in 1572
that Sir Henry Killigrew, the English Agent in
Scotland, recorded his often-quoted observa-
rion as to the nobles and burgesses " taking
more on them," and from this time forward it

was with the " Estaite of the Commoune
Peple " that the Scottish monarchs had to
reckon.

In the preceding lectures we have considered
the homes of the first two of these three orders,
examining the castle of a feudal lord in the
fifteenth century, and the manse of a Pre-
Reformation priest in the sixteenth. It is
fitting that we should now turn to the homes of
the burgesses, of whose rise to influence and of
whose advance in domestic comfort the records
of the time supply clear evidence. Let us glance,
therefore, for a few moments at the domestic
surroundings of Frances Spottiswood, a cloth
merchant who died in Edinburgh about 1540.
One incident of his career is recorded, and is
worth mentioning because of the picture it
calls up of a sight which often met the eyes of
townsmen in those unsettled times. He is
named in the Edinburgh Burgh Records as one
of a small group of citizens who, in 1521,
appeared before a notary and formally protested
against the " takin doun of the ii heids of the
chalmerlane and his brother of the tolbuth
end," and refused to be responsible for the
consequences of the removal of those ghastly
trophies.

The merchant's booth, where he plies his
trade wearing a brown doublet with scarlet
hose, and girt with a silken belt from which

hangs a purse with gold tassels, occupies the ground-floor of his house, and the entrance to the dwelling-house above is by an outside fore-stair. Ascending these steps we find ourself in the hall or principal room, where an arras " hingar " or hanging covers one wall, and the long table has a covering which is also of tapestry. The lower half of the two small windows is shuttered instead of glazed, and in the shutters oval holes are cut to allow the occu-pants to thrust their heads through and watch the street life below. The merchant's own chair stands at one end of the table, while there is a form for his wife and young son. At one side stands a double counter, and on this may be set out some of the larger tin dishes and, more prominently placed, a silver maser, a silver " piece " or cup, and a silver salt-cellar enriched with gold. These and a set of a dozen silver spoons testify to the burgess' prosperity. The smaller trenchers and other tin dishes are kept in a vessel-aumrie, where also are folded away the dornick tablecloth, napkins and towels. The furniture is not of a merely rough and utilitarian kind, for there is a carved oak meat-aumrie and an oak settle also richly carved. Here too is kept his " stand of harness " or suit of armour, with a jack and steel bonnet and a two-handed sword ; for a merchant or craftsman had to be a good man at arms, and was required to be ready to take his part in defending the community from violence. Belongings of a more personal kind are an ivory stamp or seal tipped with silver, a gold signet ring, an ivory rosary and a gold pendant in the form of a head of St. John.

Adjoining the hall is the bedchamber, where there is a large stand bed fitted with curtains of, " say," a serge-like cloth sometimes containing a little silk, and a bedcover of arras ; while a " futegang " or step was arranged by the side of the bed. There is also a press containing two closed receptacles in which clothes can be laid, and, as further provision for clothes and bed-linen, a large " schryne " or box, and a travelling chest which may have accompanied the cloth-merchant on his visits to Flanders. A sponge and comb are mentioned, the sponge here meaning a brush, and a towel hung on a pin on the wall ; the only basin mentioned is " ane hali watter fat " or holy water basin. Along with these there is a mirror—perhaps the earliest mention of a mirror as a piece of bedroom furniture in Scottish records. A spinning-wheel and implements for wool carding tell us of the home employments of the merchant's wife, who seems to have been considerably younger than her husband, for after his death at a good old age she married again.

Among other significant possessions of Spottiswood were a horse with a plough, " ane par of harrowis," a cart and sledge and other agricultural implements. These remind us that the towns were still rural communities largely dependent on the cultivation of the " town acres " on their outskirts, and the cloth-merchant had no doubt an allotment of the common land on the usual nineteen years' lease.

In the booth below there is a low curtain of arras used to partition off part of the room, a " burd till lay claith apone " and other suitable provision for his trade, including a ward-aumrie and several chests for storing goods. There are also three items of more artistic interest. The first of these is a painted and gilded image of Our Lady. The second is described as " Sanct James Staf with ane slap." A slap, or slop, ordinarily means a riddle or sieve, but seems here to be applied to the reticulated form of wallet associated with the staff which is the emblem of St. James the Greater. The patron saints of the various gilds varied in different towns, but St. James does not seem to have been associated with any of the Edinburgh trades, St. John the Baptist, whose head Spottiswood wore as a pendant, being the patron of the tailzeours. There was, however, an altar to St. James in St. Giles' Cathedral, and this was under the charge of the

Provost, Bailies and Council of Edinburgh, and the emblem may have been carried by Spottiswood in the town processions.

The third, and most interesting, item is " ane hingand brod of oley cullouris." This cannot have been a signboard, as though trade signs of various sorts were in use even in the fifteenth century, boards with signs painted on them were unknown till early in the seventeenth. " Brod " is the word regularly used for a picture. We read, for instance, in the royal inventories, of the " brod of the pictour of the Quene Regent brocht out of France," and of " aucht paintit broddis, Doctouris of Almaine " (1561). The " brod of oley cullouris," then, seems to have been a picture, and it is interesting as a very early instance of the possession of an oil painting in a private house in Scotland. The portraits of James III, still in Holyrood, of James IV, attributed to Holbein, and even that of James V, in the possession of the Duke of Devonshire, were all, of course, painted before this date ; and there are many early references to painting. On examination, however, these will be found to apply to something other than pictures in oil colour. Thus, in 1450, St. Salvador's College at St. Andrew's had a " new paynted clayth of Sant Lorans, abwn St. Michaellys alter," and many similar entries might be quoted. But these were painted hangings intended as substitutes for tapestry, and they were painted not in oils but with pigments soluble in water. Such hangings are referred to in Shakespeare's *Henry IV*, where he speaks of " Slaves as ragged as Lazarus in the painted cloth." Another set of early references, such as that to David Pratt, who painted the altar at Stirling in 1497, and another which speaks of " ane ymage of St. Katryn, new pantyt be the Prouest " in 1450, may also be set aside. It would be pleasant to conceive a Scottish Provost spending cloistral hours in executing a *primitif* portrait of St. Catherine, but it is likely that his actual work consisted in recoating with rather gaudy colours a carved figure of the saint. But Spottiswood's brod was a picture in the modern sense, and it is likely that he may have acquired it himself in Flanders, and may thus have been one of the earliest, if not actually the first, private patron of the art of painting in Scotland. The interest that the early merchants had in the fine arts may be traced in Wedderburn's *Compt Buik*, where we find him noting that " John Meill has promyttit a fyn gilt brod with a pictour, how sone he passes to France," and, on another occasion, that " Thomas Young is awin me 2 payntit brodis ouergilt at his hame-cuming from Flanders." The taste for pictorial art soon began to diffuse itself, and in 1585 a Dutch painter called

Adrian Vanyone was made a burgess of Edinburgh " to be employed in his craft in the town and to instruct apprentices."

Such a house as we have been examining is interesting because it affords a glimpse of the home life of the burgher class which was to produce such men as Robert Gourlay and George Heriot. It enables us to see why it was in the homes of the burgesses, rather than in the castles of the nobles, that the way was being prepared for the great changes in domestic life that were to be introduced in the reign of James VI. The burgess lived in a comparatively small house with his own family, and only one or two servants or apprentices to complete the household. In these conditions the transition towards the modern conception of a life of domestic privacy was easier and more natural than among the nobles, living with considerable retinues in their mediæval castles, and maintaining a certain state which tended to perpetuate the feudal tradition. Spottiswood's house, consisting of only two or three rooms, is furnished with a sense of the artistic value of furniture in adding a beauty and dignity to home life ; and such a sense is not often found in the castles of the time. The silver spoons and vessels, the napery and toilet accessories, all point to a certain fastidiousness in the details of indoor life, and an exacting standard in these matters was more easily acquired in the towns than in the country. The burgesses too were in closer touch with the refinements introduced by foreign trade, and had opportunities of picking up novelties and improvements in the equipment and arrangement of the house which were slower in reaching the nobles in their country homes ; while the freer intercourse of town life led to the circulation of new ideas and the rapid adoption of new fashions. Finally, the prosperous tradesman had this advantage over the nobles, that he had a command of money which enabled him to indulge and cultivate his tastes and so, thanks to his foreign connections, to become a pioneer in introducing works of art and other products of countries whose civilisation was more advanced.

The mirror already spoken of is probably an instance of the additions to domestic convenience introduced by the burgesses. Mirrors are mentioned as having been bought for the King in 1503, but one of these was " bocht at the cremare," that is from a pedlar, and another picked up in Dumfries for eightpence, so that they appear to have been cheap trifles hawked about the country. They were probably curious toys rather than satisfactory reflectors. It is not till 1578 that we find mirrors mentioned in the royal inventories, Queen Mary having " ane fair steill glas " and a small faceted mirror described as " ane uther less, schawing monie faces in the visie." In the following century, when they came into more general use, they were known as " keiking glasses "—a name which suggests that they were still only of small size and perhaps that their use was still rather furtive and occasional than established by custom. The old song says

> Sweet Sir, of your courtesie,
>   When ye come by the Bass then,
> For the love ye bear to me
>   By me a keiking glass then 1

The use of clocks in the house is also due to the middle-class townsmen, who were the first to feel the need of punctuality in keeping appointments and in regulating their business. Even the alarm clock existed in Scotland as early as 1564, when the good ship *Neptune* arrived at Burntisland, having on board, among other goods said to have been taken " in piracie," " ane litill knok with ane walknar (wakener) ouregilt." Other novelties which appeared about that time were introduced through the Court, whose relations with France kept it in touch with the latest developments there. Fans, for instance, were used by Queen Mary, and they are described as " culing fannis of litle wandis," while a forerunner of the modern parasol may perhaps be found in " ane litle cannabic of crammasie satyne of thrie quarter lang, furnisit with freinyes and fassis (fringes and tassels) made of gold and crammasie silk ; monie litle paintit buttons ; all seruing to bear to mak schadow befoir the Queen." Other familiar articles that first came into use in the sixteenth century include shoehorns, then called shoeing horns, which are mentioned in 1522 ; and glass vessels and cups, which, though still a rarity, are referred to in 1526. Among certain small gear in a great box belonging to a burgess of the " nobill burgh of Abirdene " we find " spectikyllis " named in 1546, but these were probably in use a hundred years earlier, as we know them to have been in England.

An inventory of the possessions of Sir David Lyndsay, of the Mount, is preserved in the Register of Acts and Decreets, and it has some interesting features. Among his silver, for instance, we find " ane dusoun of silver spunis havand the armis of the said umquhile Schir David thairon," perhaps the earliest record of a private owner having his silver so marked. Heraldic zeal, however, need not surprise us in one who was Lyon King of Arms and author of the *Register of Scottish Arms*. Even more interesting is the fact that he left " ane byble in Inglis," for Lyndsay, though a reformer with a singularly unbridled tongue, died within the communion of the Church. Many English versions of the Bible had been published before Lyndsay's death in 1555, but it was not till twenty-four years later that the first version printed in Scotland, by Bassendyne and Arbuthnott, was issued. And though the Edinburgh Town Council decreed in the following year that all " substantious houshalderis " must have a Bible in their houses, it is not till early in the seventeenth century that we find them appearing as usual family possessions.

That native wood-carvers were to be found in Scotland even before the close of the fifteenth century is shown by the accounts for the work done at Stirling Castle. Payments are entered as made " to Dauid, kervour, in erlis for the gallory quhilk he suld mak for x merkis " and " to the kervour that took in task the siling of the chapel." The fact that the panelling or " siling " was entrusted to a carver seems to show that it was definitely artistic work and not mere carpentry. But such work was confined for the most part to ecclesiastical interiors. The scarcity of oak, apart from other causes, made domestic panelling much less common than in England. " Syllit chalmers " were often rooms whose walls or roofs were merely faced with boarding. Even as late as 1622, when the standard of domestic decoration had advanced considerably, the Englishman, John Ray, wrote,

" In the most stately and fashionable houses, in great towns, instead of ceiling, they cover the chambers with firr boards, nailed on the roof within side " And, indeed, this squalid fashion may be seen to this day in some of our important Scottish Castles.

In many a church, however, there was wood-carving of a more or less ambitious kind, which kept a certain technical standard before the eyes of the people. The screen and stalls of King's College, Aberdeen, and the stalls in Dunblane, to name two instances which have survived the iconoclasm of the Reformers, and the elaborate gallery in Pitsligo Parish Church, erected in 1634, show that both before and after the Reformation there was no difficulty in providing Scottish buildings with woodwork which was both capably designed and competently executed.

The principal example of a Scottish domestic ceiling panelled in oak is the gallery at Crathes Castle. Of panelled walls there are naturally more frequent examples, but early specimens have often been mutilated as a result of their having been moved from one house to another, and ruthlessly cut to adapt them to their new situation. One fine piece of early panelling latterly formed the partition of a cowhouse ; and at Inverugie Castle a carved and gilded heraldic panel was found serving as part of a pig-trough l

Panels decorated with the " linen-fold " and the " parchment " patterns, both late Gothic types of ornament, are not unusual in Scotland. We also find examples of a type of panel carved with a floral design, a good specimen of which is the set of panels from an old house in Montrose, and now the property of Mr. P. W. Campbell, W.S. (Plate IV). The panels are believed to be the remains of a set of twenty-two, and they are supposed to be part of the fittings of Abbot Panter's Hospital, which was built in Montrose in 1516. The designing of the various subjects is well done and shows a certain resource in adapting the plant forms to the spaces to be filled. Yet the work has a somewhat sturdy and heavy-handed quality which suggests that they are rather the work of some honest Scot, discovering and, on the whole, surmounting the difficulties of design, than of a foreign workman with all the experience of the Flemish gilds at his finger ends. As to the date, the carving might pass for fifteenth-century work, but the panels in which monks are satirically represented as foxes and swine probably point to a date nearer that of the Reformation. The mouldings, cut in the solid wood of the framework, and intersecting so as to form mitres at the upper corners, but abutting on the rail at the bottom, support the later date, and suggest that the work may not be earlier than the second quarter of the sixteenth century.

Along with these panels there was found a door containing panels of similar design and workmanship, but separated by stiles ornamented with niches and representations of traceried windows. The mouldings are treated in the same way as in the panelling, and it is evident that doors and panelling were originally in the same room.

At Ethie Castle there is a cabinet associated with the name of Cardinal Beaton, who is said to have lived there after succeeding to the Abbacy of Arbroath ; the doors forming the front contain panels of very elaborate Gothic tracery. This is similar to the tracery found in French furniture of the end of the 'fifteenth century, though the horizontal openings in the upper panels of the right hand door are very unusual.

Of a totally different type are some panels which belong to Mrs. Dunn, Castledouglas, whose father, the late Mr. Joseph Train, F.S.A. (Scot.), left a MS. note in which he says that these panels were part of a " massy oaken bedstead well authenticated to have been the principal one of the Castle of Threave, and said to have been that of the Black Douglas himself. It is one of the old closet kind of bed." As the figures wear costume of the sixteenth century,

CARVED OAK PANELS FROM MONTROS
Property of P. W. Campbell, Esq., W.S.

the association with the Black Douglas may be dismissed. Unfortunately the carved work has been made up into a piece of furniture which is altogether incongruous with the age to which the carving belongs. These figures, however, though of a rather rude type, are extremely spirited, and they show us performers on the bagpipes and the fiddle, as well as archers, dancers and other types of the time, all represented with a certain alertness of observation and with considerable humour. The door from Amisfield Castle is said to be of the same type of work, but this cannot be verified till the National Museum of Antiquities has its exhibits restored to it. If true it seems to point to the existence of an untrained native artist in Dumfries and Galloway in the sixteenth century, whose work was highly unconventional and whose verve and animal spirits we can still appreciate.

At Balfour House, in Fife, there is a set of panels[1] which is of greater artistic and historical interest than any of these. There are eight large panels, extending across the end of a large room, where they have been placed above the level of the doors. They are evidently of Flemish workmanship of the end of the first quarter of the sixteenth century, and they are excellent specimens of mediæval woodcarving of a very rich and accomplished kind. The first panel, on

[1] See Plates V and VI

the left, shows the Annunciation, the Virgin kneeling at a " lettron " (lutrin), overwhelmed by the angel's message ; the pot of lilies, the descending dove, and some Gothic scroll and canopy work complete the decoration of the panel. Next comes a panel whose subject is the " Jesse tree." Jesse is shown recumbent below, while from him springs the tree bearing his descendants and culminating in the Virgin and Child at the top. The third is a sacred heraldic panel, the shield being charged with the emblems of the Passion, while two angels act as supporters ; on the helm is the crown of thorns ; the scourge, the crowing cock and other emblems occur in the crest. After this we have a panel with the arms of Cardinal Beaton and a pastoral staff ; and below are the arms of the Cardinal's father, John Beaton, and his mother, Elizabeth Monipenny, of Kinkell, the whole surrounded with a beautiful design of pomegranates. The fifth panel is carved with the Scottish arms, beneath which a thistle is introduced between the supporters. The sixth and seventh have decorative designs of various plant forms, among which the rose and the thistle are employed ; while the eighth panel is ornamented with an arrangement of carved bosses with heraldic and other motives.

The wood carving, as well as the designing, is of a high standard, such as was secured by

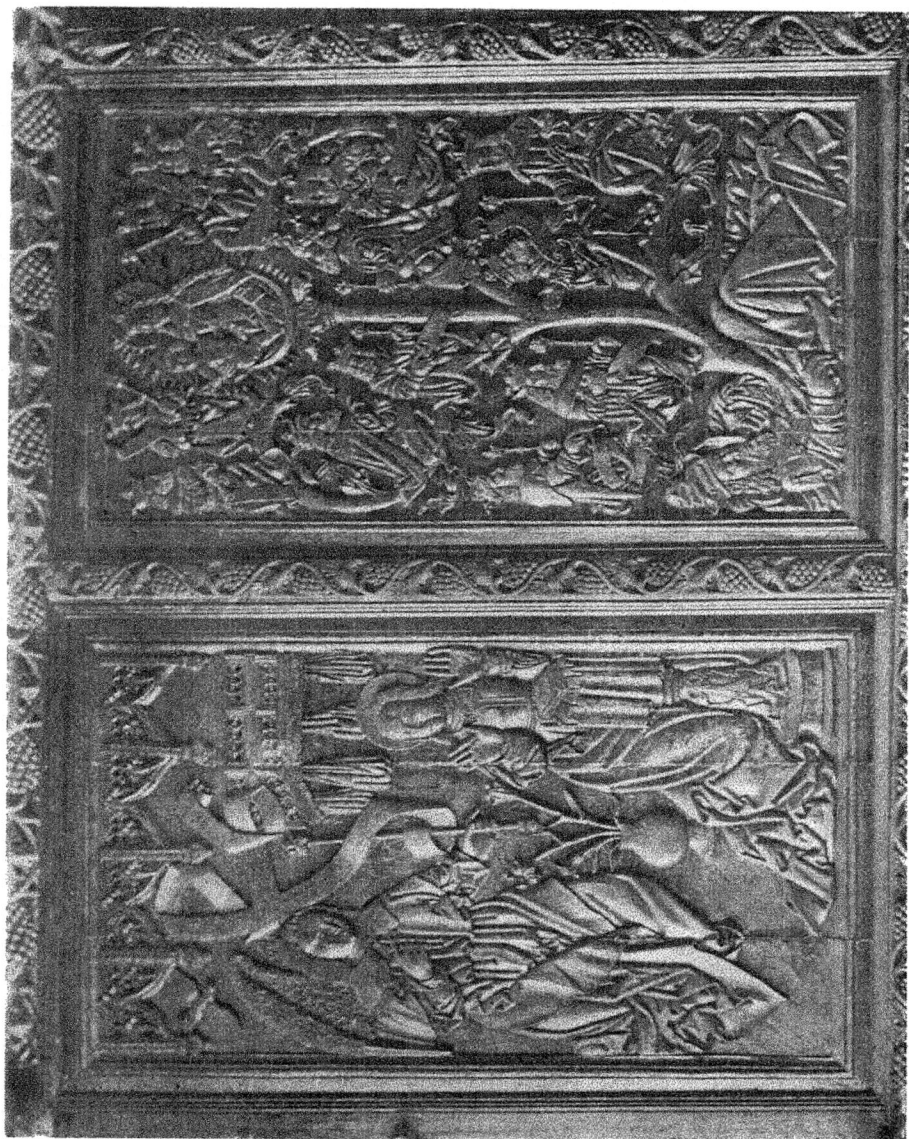

the strict control exercised by the Flemish gilds over the work turned out by their members. The work, has of course, been executed in accordance with specifications supplied by Beatoun, and the heraldic details and the Scottish emblems employed in the decoration give it a personal and national character.

The use of the pastoral staff in the fourth panel shows that the panels were executed before 1537, when, as Bishop of Mirepoix, Beatoun became entitled to display the crozier instead of the humbler emblem. As Abbot of Arbroath he had the right to the pastoral staff from 1524, and it is probable that the work was commissioned by him shortly after his appointment. The tradition in the family was that the panels had been " in the form of a canopy," and that they had formed part of the Cardinal's stall at Rome, though it was evident to the later descendants that the connection with Rome could not be seriously maintained. There can be little doubt that they were part of the decoration of a series of stalls in Arbroath Abbey, and were originally surmounted in the usual way with overhanging canopies. The bosses on the eighth panel, which is not one of the original set, have probably been taken from the carved canopies which formerly topped the stalls. It is worth noting that there are seven of these bosses, corresponding to the number of

6

the other panels, and the larger size of the central boss may imply that the panel bearing the Scottish arms occupied the central position in the original arrangement. The present arrangement is that which was made about 1670, when the panels were removed from their canopied setting and disposed on the wall so that the more interesting panels are next the light. Even as we see them to-day they are a most interesting survival of the " excellent work " which beautified the sacred buildings of Scotland, and of which so little survived the latter half of the sixteenth century, when they " broke down the carved work thereof at once with axes and hammers."

The art of ornamental needlework, or embroidery, is of very early origin, and it was no doubt in use in Scotland, though in comparatively rude forms, long before we have any record of it. By the fifteenth century it was a well-matured art, employed in decorating costume, curtains and draperies of all sorts. An embroiderer, called a browdstar, brusoure or brodinster, was one of the regular servants of the royal retinue, and many noble families also had their own embroiderers. The royal browdstar's duties included keeping the chapel vestments in order, making good the wear and tear of the tapestry hangings, and doing such odd

CARVED OAK PANELS 1   BALFOUR HOUSE.   NOS. 2 AND 4

jobs as " making a chamlot bag to the King,"
for which " Gely brousoure " was paid six
shillings by the Lord High Treasurer in 1474.
His services were valued at twenty pounds for
three terms, and he was supplied besides with
the necessary materials for his work. In the
inventory made in 1488 of the effects of King
James III, particulars are given of the drapery
of a bed, consisting of covering, roof and pen-
dicles, or curtains, all made of " variand purpur
tartar, browdin with thrissillis and a unicorne "
which by the way is perhaps the earliest reference to the thistle as the Scottish national badge
or emblem. Such work as this no doubt fell to
the royal embroiderer, with occasional trained
assistance for special work ; and the enrichment
of such bed-hangings, cloths of estate, and the
royal robes and chapel vestments must have
called for a high standard of workmanship as
well as for untiring industry.

It was in ecclesiastical ornament, however,
that needlework found its most elaborate development, and it was probably in it that
" ymagerie," or pictorial representation, was
first employed. In 1450 the High Altar at St.
Salvador's College, St. Andrews, had a " blew
claith wellowis (velvet) browdyn with ymagis
abuff the altar," and a similar cloth under the
altar (a nether frontal), " brusyt with thre
ymages of gold " ; while among other " clay-

this for the kyrk " there was " ane frontale of clayth of gold contenand the xii Appostilis."

When, in the sixteenth century, it became usual to panel the principal rooms in important houses, and tapestry passed into temporary eclipse, the change soon led to a new development of the embroiderer's art. The occupants of such rooms, we may conjecture, began to find that, with all the practical advantages of panelling, rooms so treated were somewhat dull and cheerless to live in. Tapestrie chambers had not only been rich in colour, but they had appealed to the imagination of those who lived in them by the romantic suggestion of the stories that they pictured. All this was gone, and people looked back to the brightness and poetry of the fashion that had been displaced. No doubt when the Reformation led to the churches being despoiled of their richly embroidered cloths and vestments, many of these found their way into private houses and were used to relieve the sombre austerity of panelled rooms. The same movement, however, had deprived the professional embroiderers of the principal outlet for their most important work. And it is hardly fanciful to suppose that these conditions explain the introduction of pictures stitched in coloured wools and silks, and representing biblical and romantic stories, which came into fashion towards the end of the sixteenth century. These pictures are generally small in scale, being often worked on horizontal lengths of canvas measuring about $22\frac{1}{2}$ inches in height. The length of the various pieces composing a set often varies considerably, and this suggests that they were hung in sequence, as a sort of running frieze, at a suitable level on the wall, and that the length of the separate pieces may have been determined by the width of the wall-spaces they were intended to occupy. The work is done in *petit point*, consisting of small diagonal stitches corresponding to the mesh of the canvas on which they are sewn. In most cases there are about seventeen or eighteen stitches to the vertical linear inch, and rather fewer, say fourteen to seventeen, to the horizontal inch. An interesting fact has been noted by Mr. C. E. C. Tatersall, that where two members of the design are intended to be of the same size, they correspond in actual size rather than in the number of stitches ; from which it would seem that the design has been drawn on the canvas, not copied by a count from squared paper, as is done to-day.

It was probably by women, who spent so much of their time indoors, that the want of such pictures was most felt, and much of the work itself was well fitted to appeal to the taste and domestic industry of women, even if they had not the trained capacity of the professional embroiderers. Catherine de Medici in France, Queen Elizabeth in England and Queen Mary in Scotland were all accomplished workers at embroidery. Whether any one of them was capable of producing *petit point* panels of romantic figure-subjects with backgrounds rich with ornamental gardens, architecture and every kind of animal life, is questionable. Certainly from the point of view of design, these panels were beyond the capacity of even talented amateurs. But Catherine de Medici, who, as Brantôme tells us, used to work at her silk embroidery after dinner, had her work designed, and probably supervised, by Frederic de Vinciolo, who is described as " *dessinateur des plus renommés pour broderie.*" As for Queen Mary, a letter (July, 1557) from Sir Nicholas Throkmorton to Queen Elizabeth, whose emissary he was, describes a visit to the Queen of Scots shortly after her imprisonment in Loch Leven, and mentions that she had applied for " an imbroderer to drawe furthe such works as she would be occupied about." Whether this request was granted does not seem to be recorded. The request shows her dependence on a professional designer. We learn from a French source, however, that among the servants who were taken from her by Sir Amyas Poulet in 1587 was " son brodeur, Charles Plouvart." And looking for confirmation of this to the list preserved in the State Papers concerning Queen Mary (No. 378) of the servants to whom passports were issued on their repatriation, we find the name of Charles " Plonart," probably a mistake for Plouart, the nature of whose service however is not there specified.

So deeply has the popular imagination been impressed by the romantic story of Queen Mary spending the bitter hours of imprisonment at her embroidery, that there is a tendency to attribute to her, or at least to associate with her, any piece of early embroidery that has come down through several generations of a Scottish family. One piece of work which has been exhibited more than once as belonging to, if not worked by her, is plainly of the time of Charles I ; and even much later pieces than this have been attributed to her. All such attributions should be suspected, and the intrinsic and documentary evidence carefully examined.

One specimen of her work whose authenticity can hardly be doubted is preserved at Hardwick Hall (Plate VII). The spaces formed by the interlacing design are filled with the Lily of France, the Thistle of Scotland and the Rose of England, while on the round panel in the centre the letters of the name Maria have been worked into a monogram and are surmounted with a crown. While the design is a simple one and hardly beyond the power of an amateur designer, there are one or two features—such as the little spiral which occurs between the reticulations—which may point to a more experienced hand, possibly that of Plouvart. Another panel in the possession of the Duke of Devonshire which is attributed to Queen Mary bears in the centre a scutcheon with the arms of Lady Shrewsbury, the well-known Bess of Hardwick, in the custody of whose fourth husband Mary was placed. Round the scutcheon, whose length seems to have been added to as if by an afterthought, there is a well-distributed *verdure* pattern, the leaves and flowers being comfortably adapted to the broken out line of the cartouche in which the scutcheon stands.

From embroidered work of this kind it is a far cry to the *petit point* hangings in which all the significant episodes of some romantic story are set forth, the figures wearing contemporary costume and decked with jewels and sumptuous patterned fabrics, and the whole drama set in a background in which every curiosity of nature and art is employed to enrich the effect of the whole. Such work must have taxed the skill of the most expert professional embroiderers. Consider the difficulty, for instance, of interpreting with the needle an

intricately brocaded silk or velvet draped in folds on a figure in action, where the pattern is constantly broken and distorted by the folds of the drapery, and the colours of the materials have to be perpetually modified to express the light and shade of the puckered fabric. Work so complicated must have demanded not only a highly cultivated sense of drawing, but also an undivided and concentrated attention in carrying out the design, which could hardly have been expected of Queen Mary, with so many sad and anxious thoughts to muse over as she plied her needle.

Two *petit point* panels which were acquired by Sir Noel Paton at the Murthly Castle sale are now in the Royal Scottish Museum. They are said to represent (a) *Solomon and the Queen of Sheba*, and (b) *Queen Elizabeth receiving an Embassy with a Proposal of Marriage 'from Philip II of Spain* (1559) ; the two panels are of the same height, and though one is some eight inches longer than the other the composition is so similar that they appear to be intended as a pair, in which case the subjects are rather oddly assorted, and the smaller panel perhaps represents some sixteenth-century historical subject.

The panels mounted on a screen and representing the *Story of Rehoboam* have been exhibited on several occasions since they came into the possession of Mr. Scott Moncrieff's family. These hangings were very naturally identified with the set, illustrating the same unusual subject, which appears in the inventory made in 1561 of effects belonging to Mary of Guise, and also in the list of goods handed over to James VI in 1578. Investigation, however, showed that a Rehoboam set was recorded in the earlier inventories of 1539 and 1542, and Mr. Scott Moncrieff at once recognised the probability that Mary of Guise's set was the same as that mentioned in the earlier documents, as existing at a date clearly too early for the costume in his own set. He also made a detailed inquiry into the costume in his set, and reached the conclusion that it was probably of a date later, though not much later, than 1561. There is another point. The Rehoboam hangings in the royal inventories are grouped with many others as " Tapestryis," a term properly applied to woven hangings ; and it appears very unlikely that, especially in the Scottish Court, whose vocabulary in such matters closely followed the French usage, small embroideries sewn with the needle would be so described. No doubt the word tapestry was used with a certain latitude, for we read of " ellevin tapestrie of gilt ledder " ; but where woven tapestry was not intended, I think the distinction would be clearly expressed. That the tapestries in the royal inventories were hangings of considerable size is further shown by the fact that many of them were eventually made down into bed-covers and bed-curtains, as appears in the list of beds handed over to James VI as " pertening to his hienes' derrest moder."

But though it would have added a historical interest if these hangings could have been identified with the tapestries which belonged to Mary of Guise, still their beauty and interest are inherent and do not depend on documentary evidence. They are undoubtedly of the period of Queen Mary. They came into the present owner's family in 1692, having previously belonged to another Scottish family, so that their early association with Scotland is un-doubted, and is confirmed by the use of the thistle as a piece of decoration in the uppermost panel. The number of Scottish houses in the sixteenth century likely to have such finely wrought embroideries was limited, and when we reflect that the story of Rehoboam is one that deals with a royal house in its relations to changes in the national faith, it is by no means improbable that the hangings may have had some connection with Queen Mary, whom such questions of royal policy so closely affected.

Another set of *petit point* hangings tradi-tionally attributed to Queen Mary is that be-longing to the Earl of Morton ; and its uninterrupted ownership, from the sixteenth century to the present day, by Regent Morton and his descendants might well seem to support the tradition. But, in the first place, it is impossible that work of such rare beauty and such intricate richness could have been produced by Mary and her ladies, and above all at Loch Leven where there was no artist to execute the design. Mary was only eleven months in Loch Leven. By June, 1568, she had left Scotland. Though it is extremely difficult to deduce an exact time from costume, still the costumes in these hangings appear to be later, rather than earlier, than 1568; and if this is so they are hardly likely, supposing them to have been worked by Queen Mary, to have come to Scotland and into the hands of Regent Morton. (Plate VIII).

But there is one line of investigation which might lead to interesting results. While most of the *petit point* hangings of the period have a strong resemblance to each other in their general character, one finds on comparison that the various examples differ from each other just as sharply as do, for instance, the drawings by different artists in *Punch*. After careful examination of a large number of such needlework hangings I have found none comparable in draughtsmanship, in the expressive grace and romantic dignity of the figures, and in the resourceful inventiveness of the garden back-

PLATE I

ground, with Lord Morton's set. So remarkable are these qualities that one asks who there was among contemporary artists who could have produced such work ? And one remembers the name of Nicholas Hilliard, goldsmith and portrait painter to Queen Elizabeth, of whom Donne wrote :

> A hand or eye
> By Hilliard drawn is worth a historye
> By a worse painter made.

I do not know that there is any evidence that Hilliard designed for embroidery, but it is quite likely that the members of the Broderers' Company, incorporated by Queen Elizabeth in 1561, may have applied to the leading artists of the time to supply designs for the *petit point* panels that just then came into fashion. Hilliard has left a considerable number of miniatures, and there is a couple of drawings by him at the British Museum, one of which is the design for the Great Seal of Ireland ; but there is nothing in these to justify one in attributing the design of the Morton hangings to him. One of the best known of the miniatures is that representing George Clifford, Earl of Cumberland, as Queen's Champion ; and in this the Champion's scutcheon bears a device consisting of a globe, representing the earth, between a sun " in his splendour "—that is surrounded with rays—in the upper part of the field, and a moon and stars in the lower part. This may be some flattering allusion to Elizabeth, and it is worth noting that the seated figure, which might well be a portrait of Queen Elizabeth, in the central panel of Lord Morton's hangings, wears shoulder pieces showing the device of a sun in his splendour. In connection with this figure and its garden surroundings we may recall Hilliard's description of how, when he " first came in her Highnes presence to drawe," the Queen, in order to avoid all shadows on the face " chosse her place to sit in . . . the open ally of a goodly garden, where no tree was neere, nor anye shadowe at all." If these hangings should represent a series of scenes in some masque written in honour of Elizabeth and perhaps acted at court, it might well have been depicted by Hilliard as painter to the Queen. There are passages in his *Arte of Limning* in which Hilliard makes it plain that designing of this kind was known to him, though he does not explicitly say that he practised it. He naturally, as a miniature painter, claims a higher place for that art " as a thing apart from all other painting or drawing, and tendeth not to comon mens vsse, either for furnishing of howsses or any *patternes for tapistries* "; and elsewhere he speaks of portraiture as a thing " which indeed one should not atempt vntill he weare metly good in story work." It is a fair inference that he had some experience in designing such story work as is exemplified in these hangings.

Hilliard devoted much attention to the rendering of jewellery, and in this respect and in all the opulent detail with which every inch of the hangings is covered, the design might very well be that of a goldsmith. But besides such general considerations there are historical facts which seem to support the hypothesis of his connection with this piece of needlework, or which at least make such a connection plausible. In the course of a search into the beginnings of industrial enterprise in Scotland I chanced on this curious and interesting fact, which seems to have escaped the notice of Hilliard's biographers. In the year 1580 a company of adventurers came to Scotland with the object of working gold mines in Crawfurd Muir, Lanarkshire, where alluvial gold had been found by earlier enthusiasts. The head of this company was Nicholas Hilliard, who had with him Arnold Bronkhorst, a Flemish painter, as his assistant. It was to Regent Morton that application had to be made for a patent to work the mines, and it seems probable that the applicants would come bearing gifts for those whose favour had to be won. What more likely than that Hilliard should bring a set of these hangings, which were the latest fashion in the great English houses, and which were easily packed up and carried ?

Regent Morton refused to grant the concession, although we are told that "the said Bronkhorst became a suitor at least for the space of four moneths and did not prevail unto this day." Hilliard had meanwhile returned to England having " lost all his chardges and never since got any recompence, to Mr. Hilliard's great hinderance, as he saith, who yet liveth, and confirmeth the same." So Steven Atkinson tells us in his *Discoverie and Historie of the Gold Mynes in Scotland*, published in 1619, the year of Hilliard's death. Bronkhorst, he says, " was forced to become one of his Majestie's sworne servants at Ordinary in Scotland, to draw all the small and great pictures for his Majesty " ; and an original precept at the Register House, signed by James VI, records payment to him for two portraits of the King and one of George Buchanan, with an additional one hundred marks " as an gratitude for his repairing to this countrey."

This story of the gold-mining adventurers at least suggests, as an alternative to the Loch Leven origin of the hangings, which is improbable on account of dates, how this romantic piece of needlework may have come into the possession of the family of Lord Morton. Whether it was designed by Hilliard himself cannot meanwhile be proved. The evidence of the miniatures does not support the ascription, though it is difficult to argue from portrait miniatures, where the artist is closely tied to the realities of his sitters, to storied design, where he is free to indulge his personal conceptions of ideal beauty. One clue that might lead to an identification of the designer is the treatment of the hands, which is very distinctive. The fingers are shown as curved and separated, each with its own action, and the forefinger having more upward spring from the knuckle than the others. There is a set of three small panels at the Victoria and Albert Museum where there is a somewhat similar treatment of the hands, and some of the men's heads are not unlike those in Lord Morton's panels. But the museum set lacks the elegance of drawing and the expressive beauty of the figures in the set we have been examining.

THE DECAY OF FEUDALISM AND THE DEVELOPMENT OF FAMILY LIFE

JAMES VI, 1578–1625

New conceptions of domestic life—Historical origins of the change—Passing away of feudalism—Expansion of trade and increasing importance of the towns—Enrichment of the nobles by partition of Church property—An era of building—Domestic character of the new architecture—Feudal lords transformed into courtiers, with luxurious standards of living—Changes in domestic arrangements—The hall gives place to the dining-room—The " Dravand Burd "—Table manners at Court and in private life—Table ware, etc.—Display of plate—Cupboards with " gries "—The dresser—Dessert and the banquet—The parlour—Stuffed chairs—The taffel—Books; the Family Bible—Pictures—Music—Life of the leisured classes—Men's employments and recreations—How a lady of fashion spent her day—Dietetic dangers and some medical counsels—Children's toys—A boy's penknife—Duncan's new doublet.

ALL through the sixteenth century, house furnishing in Scotland proceeded on the basis of a mediæval conception of social life. As, with more settled conditions, the country advanced in prosperity, and as the middle classes gradually gained in influence and importance, the diffusion of wealth began to be reflected in the increase of luxury in the homes of gentle and simple. Carved and gilded wood, rich fabrics and jewellery and ornaments of every kind gave the interiors of many Scottish homes an interest which they had not had in ruder and less sophisticated days. Yet, if there was more conscious art, the furniture was of the same types and served the same social usages as in the fifteenth century. Such advance as there was amounted rather to a general enrichment of the details of domestic furnishing than to any radical change in its principles.

But almost with the stroke of the new century there came a change. As we read the inventories of household plenishings of the closing years of the sixteenth century and the opening years of the seventeenth, we cannot but recognise that a great upheaval in the arrangements of household life was taking place and that innovations were being introduced that really implied a new conception of social order. In these inventories we constantly find new articles of furniture, meeting wants which were unknown to the previous generation. The interiors assume a more comfortable, and, to our modern eyes, a more familiar air than that of the somewhat severe and ceremonial apartments of the fifteenth and sixteenth centuries. Feudalism has run its course, and we are watching the beginnings of the modern world with its distinctive conception of comfort and privacy in family life.

So sudden and so striking is the change that the least reflective must turn to history for an explanation ; and, indeed, it is easy to recognise some of the influences which combined to precipitate a crisis which was already overdue.

There was in the first place the modern spirit, born of the Renaissance—a spirit which could not coexist with the feudalism of the Middle Ages, and which was bound to overturn, sooner or later, any system based on such a conception. The new independence of thought which characterised the time must in itself have led to a reconsideration of the social relations on which mediæval household life depended. It was stimulated by the freer intellectual contact with the countries of Europe both through foreign travel and as a result of the interchange of printed literature. But apart from such general causes, the Reformation, which was the crisis through which Scotland chiefly felt and responded to the Renaissance movement, had specific results which exercised a very marked and definite influence on social conditions in Scotland. The long drain of Scottish money towards Rome was now at an end, and the accumulation of capital in the country was at last possible. At the same moment traders all over the country were relieved from the competition of the Church, whose immense resources in wealth and organisation had enabled her to overshadow the business enterprises of her humbler rivals. Trade and industry, thus relieved from the burdens that had so long over-weighted them, began to expand and find their natural development. Tradesmen and crafts-men who had hitherto found shelter under the wing of the Castle or of the Abbey, and had lived at the beck and call of their feudal superiors, migrated into the towns and carried on their work under the protection of the town gilds. Thus, while the Castles lost their im-portance, the towns were every day gaining in population and in activity. It only wanted the circulation of considerable sums of money to ensure that the advance in prosperity should be confirmed and developed ; and this too came about as an indirect consequence of the Reforma-tion. In 1587 an Act of Parliament was passed which, subject to provision for the clergy, transferred all ecclesiastical property to the King—the measure being justified by the allegation that the Crown had, before the Reformation, been driven to overtax the people in order to make good its own gifts to the Church. However this may be, it is estimated that from a third to a half of the total wealth of the country had passed into the possession of the Church. From the property which was now transferred to the Crown, James made lavish gifts to the nobles, many of whom, finding themselves suddenly possessed of lands and a sufficient income, seized the opportunity of re-modelling their castles or of building new homes of a less antiquated character. As artillery, by this time, could make short work of the strongest masonry, there was no use in erecting strongly fortified keeps as in the days that were past. Nor was it any longer necessary to subordinate the actual plan and internal arrangements of the house to considerations of defence from attack, unless in remoter parts of the country where raids might still have to be provided against. Those who built new houses were therefore free for the first time to make comfort and privacy their primary consideration. Such mediæval and military features as appear in the mansions built at that time are survivals of a tradition which, though no longer suited to the needs of the age, was familiar and not easily thrown aside. What is really new and typical in the architecture of the time is its strongly domestic character.

Another effect of the erection of the lands of the ancient Church into temporal lordships is worth noting. James succeeded, by means of such gifts, in attaching the nobles to his Court and committing them to his policy. They thus insensibly passed from the position of more or less independent feudal lords to that of more or less subservient courtiers. This change gives a transitional note to the social atmosphere of the time. Sir Walter Scott points out, in his introduction to the *Fortunes of Nigel*, that " in all the comedies of the age the principal character for gaiety and wit is the young heir, who has totally altered the establishment of the father to whom he has succeeded." The comedies to which he alludes—those of Shadwell and others—are such as give a picture of English life. But the change was sharper still in Scotland ; for in addition to the influences that operated in England there was the sudden introduction of new standards of life resulting from the Union of the Crowns in 1603 and the contact it brought with a much wealthier civilisation. William Lithgow, writing in 1628, gives a rather highly coloured picture of the age : " All the gold of the kingdom is daily transported away with superfluous posting for court, whence they never return anything save spend-all, end-all ; then farewell fortune l " And he talks of " our ignoble gallants, though nobly born, swallowing up the honour of their predecessors with posting foolery, boy-winding horns, gormandising gluttony, lust and vain apparel."

On every side we have evidence of the social changes that followed from the Scottish King's accession to the English throne. The migration of all sorts of workers from the country to the towns, which had been going steadily on for a long time past, brought embarrassments of a grave kind to the country nobles, accustomed as these had been to command the services of skilled country craftsmen by a local bartering of their produce. With an advancing standard of comfort in domestic life, and an increasing dependence on the towns to supply his wants, the country noble was faced with the difficulty of converting his produce into cash, and when he paid a visit to the town he was chagrined to find himself a person of much less influence and importance than the prosperous tradesman who had a ready command of money. His hungry retinue, which he felt necessary to support his dignity, was apt not only to add to his difficulties but also to expose him to ridicule. He returned to his castle wounded and embittered, too firmly rooted in the past to be capable of adapting himself to the social changes which everywhere confronted him. Very different from the position of such a penniless feudal lord was that of those courtiers who had been enriched by sharing in the division of monastic property. These brought back from Court all kinds of new and luxurious ideas, and the castles in which they had been born and bred were condemned as unsuitable to the kind of life to which they had now become accustomed. The mediæval hall was out of date and must needs be replaced by a family dining-room. Their nostrils having become too sensitive to tolerate the smell of cooking, the kitchen had to be banished to a remoter part of the house. Drawing-rooms, parlours and studies began to be introduced, and the privacy of the upper bedrooms was secured by providing separate access to each by turret stairs, instead of letting one room lead into another as in earlier times. Now that thick walls were no longer necessary, rooms were more brightly lighted and pleasanter to live in, and though the English development of great mullioned and transomed windows never took root in Scotland, the fashion of bow windows was sometimes adopted so as to command a wider outlook from within.   The interiors too were more elaborately decorated ; the walls were often treated with wooden panelling, and the ceilings enriched with elaborate plaster ornament or, as in the long gallery at Pinkie, painted with classical or other subjects.

The changed conception of household life which is expressed in these architectural innovations is equally clearly reflected in the domestic arrangements and furnishing.   In some houses the hall became the family dining-room, though the old trestle tables with their forms might be replaced by furniture of a newer type.   In others the hall was abandoned as a " living room " and the meals and the family life in general were transferred from it to the more secluded apartments beyond. Thus the hall, which had hitherto been the main arena of the social life of the house, gradually ceased to rank as a room at all, and degenerated into what it has become in our modern houses, a mere antechamber or entrance lobby in which strangers could be allowed to wait without interfering with the privacy of the family. This process of degeneration was further accelerated when the hall was transferred from the first to the ground floor, which had hitherto been given up to vaulted cellars. Sometimes the new dining-room was in practice very little different from the old hall ; the antiquated furniture was made use of, the board being placed along the wall, with a piece of tapestry, or a painted " brod," or picture, hung on the wall behind the master's seat, to represent the old parelling. But where a family was inclined, and had the means, to adopt the new fashions without the necessity of compromise, we may conceive them dining in a panelled room, well lighted and with a pleasant outlook ; the table would be placed not by the wall but in the middle of the room, and it would be no longer a long board on trestles, but a solid wainscot or walnut table built upon turned or carved " branders " or legs, and made with two or three leaves for

extension when necessary. This was what was
called " ane drawand buird,"[1] and though
generally rectangular it was sometimes circular
in form, for we find occasional references to
" ane roundel burde with thrie leavis." Such
a table is very significant of the new social
customs which were everywhere asserting themselves. Little general conversation can have
been possible when those who dined together
sat in a row on one side of a board which might
be fifteen or twenty feet long. The new
fashion allowed the guests to sit more or less in
a circle round a roomier table whose length
could be adjusted so as to be no greater than
the number of guests required—a much more
sociable arrangement. Another change was
equally significant. At mediæval meals there
had been only one chair, as we have seen, and
this was the rightful seat of the master of the
house—a tradition which we still recognise
when we hold a meeting under the guidance of
someone who occupies " the Chair." Guests
of distinction might be provided with stools
but most of the company sat on forms. When
James IV, for instance, met his affianced bride,
Margaret Tudor, daughter of Henry VII, at
Newbattle, a contemporary writer tells us
" The tables were then drest and served. The
Kynge satt in the Chayre and the Quene abouffe

---

[1] See Plate IX.

hym on hys ryght baund. For because the Stole of the Quene was not for hyr ease, he gaffe hyr the sayde Chayre," and this is mentioned, of course, as one of the graceful and exceptional courtesies which the King showed to the English Princess. But with the passing away of feudalism the chair lost its throne-like attributes, and from the beginning of the seventeenth century we find chairs appearing in sets for family use, very often in sets of four. Thus an inventory of 1607 has " Foure chyres of walnut trie, price of the piece viij lib. Item, foure chyres of aik, price of ilk chyre iiij lib." And with these appear " aucht fyne buffeit stuillis, price of ilk stuill xl s." The use of forms for sitting on at meals was not, of course, at once abandoned when chairs had been introduced, for old habits are not so easily thrown off. But where a round table was used, forms were obviously impossible, and little by little the custom of using chairs round a table set in the middle of the room displaced the earlier usage.

We have some interesting particulars of a banquet given by James VI to the Constable of Castile at Whitehall Palace in the year 1604. After grace had been said, the King and Queen washed their hands in the same basin, while another basin served for the Prince and the chief guest. The King and Queen sat at the head of the table at some distance from each

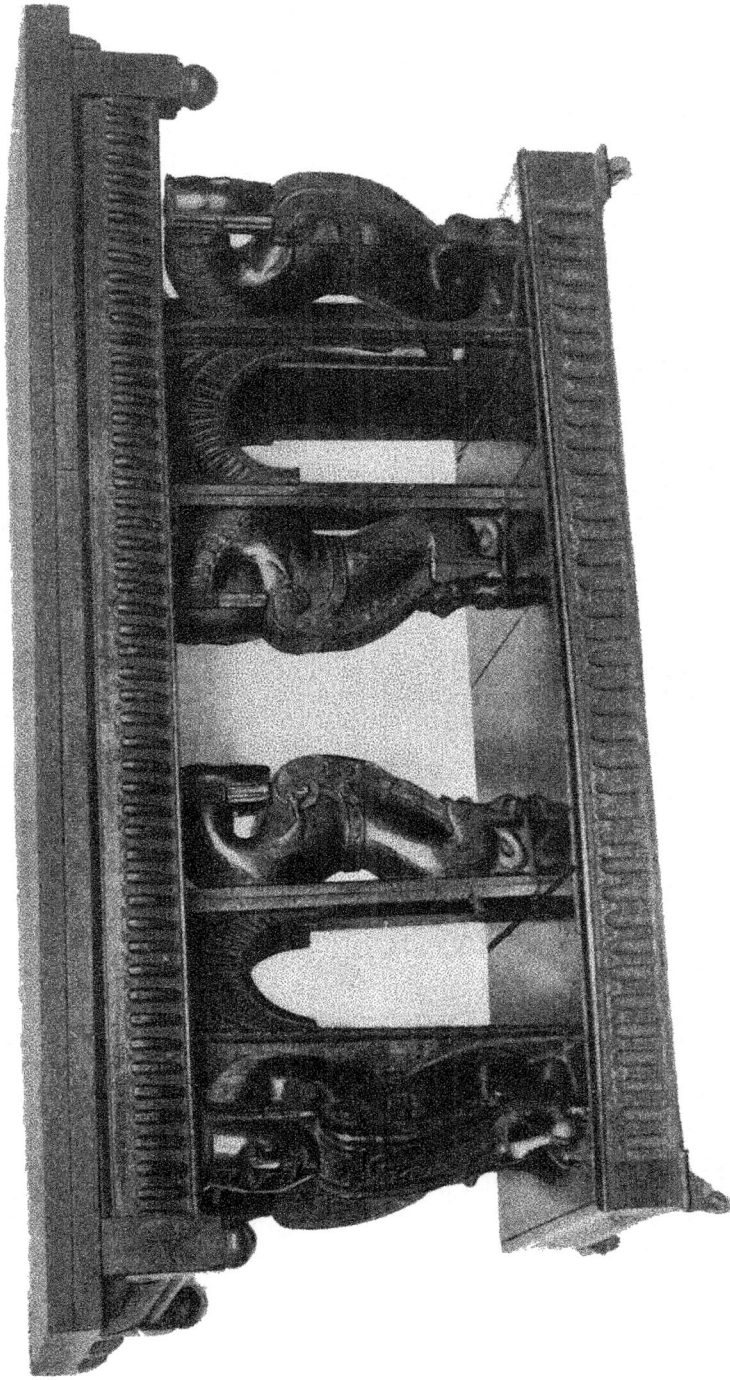

AN E DRAWAND BUIRD," OR EXTENDING TABLE.

Property of the Earl of Home

other, under the canopy of state, and on chairs of brocade with cushions. The Prince and the Constable sat on tabourets, or stools, also of brocade with cushions. At the side of the room stood a buffet laden with vessels of gold, and of agate and other precious stones. The banquet was accompanied with instrumental music. The guests had their heads covered, but when the King rose to drink to the health of the King and Queen of Spain, he uncovered his head. The banquet lasted for three hours, and then, the cloth having been removed, everyone rose up. The table, we are told, was placed upon the ground, which seems to mean that it was lifted down from the dais, " and their Majesties, standing upon it, proceeded to wash their hands, which is stated to be an ancient ceremony." Dancing followed. The candid chronicler relates that the morning after the banquet the Constable of Castile awoke with a slight attack of lumbago !

This of course was a ceremonial Court dinner given in England, and no doubt under the influence of English standards and traditions. Very considerable allowances would naturally have to be made if we were to attempt to deduce from it any general impression of the table manners of the time. Fynes Moryson, a graduate of Cambridge, who was in Scotland five years before James succeeded to the English

Crown, gives us the following picture of the
conditions of domestic life of the time, though
it must be remembered that his impressions
are derived simply from the houses of such
townsmen or countrymen as were willing to
entertain him " upon acquaintance or en-
treaty." " Touching their diet," he says, " they
cate much red Colewort and Cabbage, but little
fresh meate, using to salt their Mutton and
Geese, which made me more wonder, that they
use to cate Beef without salting. The Gentlemen reckon their revenewes, not by rents of
monie, but by chauldrons of victuals, and keep
many people in the Families, yet living most on
Corne and Rootes, not spending any great
quantity on flesh. Myself was at a Knight's
House, who had many servants to attend him,
that brought in his meate with their heads
covered with blew caps, the Table being more
than halfe furnished with great platters of
porredge (or broth), each having a little piece of
sodden meate : And when the Table was served,
the servants did sit downe with us, but the
upper messe in steede of porredge, had a
Pullet with some prunes in the broth. And I
observed no art of Cookery, or furniture of
Household stuffe, but rather rude neglect of
both, though myself and my companion, sent
from the Governour of *Barwicke* about border-
ing affairs, were entertained after their best

manner. The Scots living then in factions, used to keepe many followers, and so consumed their revenew of victuals, living in some want of money. They vulgarly ate harth Cakes of Oates, but in Cities have also wheaten bread, which for the most part was bought by Courtiers, Gentlemen, and the best sort of Citizens. . . . They drinke pure Wines not with sugar as the English, yet at feasts they put Comfits in the Wine after the French manner, but they had not our Vinteners fraud to mix their Wines. The better sort of citizens brew ale, their usuall drinke, which will distemper a strangers bodie." Taylor, the water poet, who travelled in Scotland some twenty years later, and who, though he was practically dependent on charity for his entertainment, was received at many more important houses than his predecessor, naturally gives a more flattering account of his experiences : " In Scotland, beyond Edenborough, I have been at houses like castles for building : the master of the house his beaver being his blue bonnet, one that will weare no other shirts but of the flaxe that growes on his owne ground, and of his wives, daughters or servants spinning ; that hath his stockings, hose and jerkin of the wool of his owne sheepes backes ; that never (by his pride of apparell) caused mercer, draper, silkeman, embroyderer, or haberdasher to breake

and turn bankerupt ; and yet this plaine home-
spunne fellow keepes and maintaines thirty,
forty, fifty servants, or perhaps more, every day
releeving three or four score poore peeple at his
gate ; and besides all this can give noble enter-
tainement for foure or five dayes together, to
five or six Earles and Lordes, besides Knights,
Gentlemen and their followers, if they be three
or foure hundred men and horse of them ;
where they shall not only feede but feast, and not
feast but banket. . . . Many of these worthy
housekeepers there are in Scotland, amongst
some of whom I was entertained ; from whence
I did truely gather these aforesaid observations.''

In Scottish houses the dishes used at table
were almost invariably of pewter. Well equipped
houses on a large scale had sometimes as many
as forty dozen pewter plates of various sizes,
while in a small tradesman's house it is usual to
find three or four dozen plates, saucers and
trenchers. Besides these dishes there would be
stoups of various sizes, generally holding a
quart, a pint, a chopin and a mutchkin respectively ; while drinking cups of " tree," often
with bases or pedestals of pewter or silver, were
not uncommon. One or two lavers were also
part of the ordinary table outfit. Lavers are
generally defined as basins used for washing, but
this is quite a mistake. In old documents the

laver is nearly always coupled with a basin, and the laver was the jug or ewer from which water was poured over the hands into the basin. These lavers and basins were of silver or of pewter according to the means of the owner. Table glass was still something of a rarity though a new fashion was the use of what was called a wine-cellar, fitted with " the haill flaccatis, glass and furneissing thairof." In one house of the period there were three dozen " fyne lame (loam, or earthenware) potis for desertis," but the employment of china or earthenware for table dishes was not yet introduced. The salt-fatt was generally of silver, and it stood in the middle of the table, and the division of the table into " above " and " below the salt " dates from this period and not from mediæval times, when the dais table was reserved for those of superior rank, and the others sat at side tables.

The persistence of ancient customs is well illustrated by the following description of a dinner in a farmhouse towards the end of the eighteenth century, and it will be noticed how closely many of the details correspond with the procedure at meals in the time of James VI. " At noon," we are told, " the gudewife with her maidens proceeded in the centre of the well-swept earthen floor to erect the timber or iron trestles and thereon to extend the *tafil* or

8

dinner-boards. In the better-class farmhouses the upper part of the dinner boards was covered with a linen cloth. More frequently the upper part of the table, at which sat the farmer and family, was separated from the lower part by a chalk line. Occasionally the distinction was indicated by the position of the salt-dish; those who sat above it were of the farmer's kin, those beneath it were his hirelings. When all were seated, they uncovered and bowed their heads for ' grace ' or blessing. . . . Grace said, all the males resumed their bonnets, which, summer and winter, they retained in eating. Before taking his seat the farmer washed his hands, but the hinds were expected to eat without attempting an ablution." No doubt in out-of-the-way parts of the country survivals of such table traditions might still be found.

In the description that has been quoted of a Court banquet at Whitehall, the display of gold plate on a buffet was mentioned, and in private houses in Scotland the custom of laying out the " weschel " on a suitable piece of furniture was still kept up. For this purpose the compter, or table, had, as we have seen, been superseded by, or had developed into, the cupboard. Sometimes the top of the cupboard was fitted with several steps, or stages, the number of which, according to the French usage, was limited in proportion to a man's rank. Cup-

boards with three " gries " or stages, such as
were inventoried at St. Andrew's Priory in 1565,
must have allowed of a considerable display of
plate.   In France the presence of these "*de-
grés*" seems to have distinguished the " *dressoir* " from the simpler credence, and the
dressoir was thus a more elaborate and pretentious piece of furniture, suited to the houses
of wealthy noblemen.   In Scotland the dresser
certainly existed as early as 1502, for an English
writer describing the arrangements at Holyrood says, " There was also in the sam Chammer
. . . a ryche Dressor, after the Guyse of the
Countre."   But whatever may have been done
at Court, the dresser was certainly not in common use under that name in private houses, and
except for " ane dressour for setting of stoupis "
which is mentioned as in the Great Hall of
Edinburgh Castle in 1566, the word is comparatively unknown until the reign of James VI,
when it occurs in many inventories ;   the
dressers of this period were frequently " indented," i.e. inlaid, or otherwise ornamented,
so that they were evidently important pieces of
furniture, and not of the rude type which we
now associate with the kitchen and the farmhouse.   The display of silver vessels on the
dresser had hardly the same significance that it
had in mediæval times, for it was no longer a
criterion of a man's wealth.   Money was more

plentiful than it had been, but on the other hand there were many more openings for its employment, so that there was neither the same practical necessity nor the same inducement to convert accumulated wealth into silver plate. Still the houses of the period had very commonly some ten or twenty handsome silver vessels, often gilded and engraved, including one or two masers, several salt-fatts, with cups, goblets, a number of " pieces " or bowls, a trencher, a laver and basin, and one or two dozen spoons.

I have mentioned a house which had " fyne lame potis for desertis " and the same house had, as early as 1594, " lyttil new plaitis for desert." In England the word " dessert " does not seem to have come into use till the middle of the following century, and Scotland acquired it from France direct. In its origin the word refers to the practice of removing the cloth at the end of a meal, when the table was " disserved " or cleared, and the fruits and sweets which followed were partaken of in a separate room. Like many another obsolete custom this usage is preserved in our present day speech ; for when we distinguish between two sizes of spoons by calling one a " table spoon " and the other a " dessert spoon " we imply that the dessert was not taken at the table where the meal was served. Sometimes the dessert was

called " the banquet," a name applied to any
light refreshment served between regular meals.
When James VI visited New College, St.
Andrews, and heard a disputation between the
" Bischope " and Andrew Melville, we read
that " the King, in his mother toung, maid sum
distingoes, and discoursit a whyll thairon," and
thereafter passed to the College Hall, where
there had been prepared " a banquet of wat and
dry confectiones, with all sortes of wyne,
wharat his Majestie camped veric merrilie a
guid whyll." You may still see the word
banquet used in this sense in the newspaper
reports of some municipal or other social
gathering in Scotland, at which the guests are
entertained to " a banquet of cake and wine."

The changes characteristic of the period were
not, of course, confined to the dining-room, and
indeed the parlours or withdrawing rooms that
were coming into use, and which displaced the
chamber of dais or principal bedroom to which
a few favoured guests had formerly retired after
meals, were in themselves very significant of
the new ideas of domestic life. In such rooms
the family could enjoy itself in peace, either
with or without the company of chosen guests,
and unembarrassed by the presence of all sorts
of dependents and retainers. The introduction
of chairs for family use allowed of more variety
and informality of grouping for conversation or

like purposes than had been possible when forms, settles and chests had been the only seats. It also led to development in the chairs themselves. There are frequent references about the middle of the sixteenth century to the covering of chairs with velvet, satin, and other materials—particularly in connection with the royal household. Such covering was however merely for purposes of decoration, and comfort was provided in those days by the use of separate cushions. But in James VI's time we have, among other novelties, the introduction of upholstered chairs—chairs so stuffed or padded as not to require the additional use of cushions. The earliest examples seem naturally to have been imported from abroad. In 1612 we read of " ane mekill Frenche bakit and buffit chyre," and a few years later of " twa grit bakit Inglis chyres, bust and steikit in the sait with ane cover of ledder thairin and coverit lykwise with ledder on the bak and stampit." Thus perhaps began the distinction between what we may call the dining-room and the drawing-room types of chair—the former designed for use at meals only, the latter adapted to less stereotyped attitudes and uses and affording comfort in hours of social relaxation.

Another piece of furniture that seems to have come rather suddenly into favour at this time was the Taffel. The Dutch or German origin

of the word is obvious, and the word was probably picked up and imported as a direct result
of trading with these countries. It does not
seem to have been generally adopted in England,
and its occasional use there seems to be due to
the influence of Scottish usages at court. The
Taffel, or Taiffel, was, as its name implies, a
table, but an examination of early references
shows that it was its small size, or its lightness,
that distinguished it from other tables. In
valuations of furniture its value is always comparatively low ; sometimes we read of " buird
claithis for the hallbuird, and *ane littil ane for
ane taiffelbuird*." George Tait, a burgess of
Edinburgh, had among his furniture (1622) "ane
chyre with ane bak for ane taffle " ; that is, a
chair convertible into a small table by bringing
forward on its swivels the table-top which
formed the back of the chair. From a number
of such allusions we may infer that the taffel
was in effect what is called an occasional table,
such as could be used for chess or cards, and
could be easily lifted from one part of the room
to another. The use of such light tables, with
the adoption of chairs instead of forms, indicates
the increased mobility and variety of the new
domestic life. Games could be played by the
fireside on a winter evening ; at other times the
table might be taken to the window so that ladies
might occupy themselves with needlework and

conversation at the same time and watch whatever there might be to interest them in the
world without. Houses were now often built
on sites chosen for their pleasant outlook ;
more and more attention was being paid to
gardens. Since the days when James IV had
had the walls of Stirling and Holyrood plastered
to suit the ideas of comfort of his English Queen,
the plastering of the rooms in private houses
had become usual, and the interiors were no
longer so cold and draughty as they must have
been when tapestry flapped upon stone walls ;
and it was pleasant to sit in comfort within,
enjoying a freedom and seclusion which had
been unattainable in the mediæval hall with its
dais and all the formality and the scheme of
social precedence that the dais implied.

In such rooms large cabinets or aumries[1] from
Holland now began to appear, and they were
valued not merely for the useful accommodation they supplied, but also as pieces of furniture which gave the rooms a certain beauty and
dignity. Carpets and rugs were beginning to
displace the use of bent grass to cover the floors,
though at first they were used rather as table-
covers. " Steikit green mats " are fairly often
met with, and James Melvill, who died in 1613,
had one of these, besides " Scots nedle-worke
carpetts " in his hall and chamber. Books were
beginning to play an important part in house-

[1] See Plate X.

PLATE II

INDENTED AUMRIE, KNOWN AS "QUEEN ANNA'S PRESS"
Property of Sir John Sterling Maxwell, Bart

hold life, and one significant feature in the inventories of the time is the appearance of the family Bible. The printing of Bassendyne's Bible had been completed by Arbuthnott in 1579, and a year later the Town Council of Edinburgh had ordered " all nychtbouris of this burgh, substantious house halderis, to haif ane bybill in thair houssis under the paynes contenit in the actes of Parliament maid thairanent." Accordingly it is common to find houses provided with " ane grit houss Bibill," sometimes accompanied by " ane little bybill." One Edinburgh citizen left among his possessions " ane grit bibill of Lumbard volum of the best sort and fynnest print, ouergilt, pryce thairof xl lib. Item ane uther bibill of Arbuthnots print, pryce thairof x lib. Item mair ane psalme buik, pryce x s."

Secular works included classical authors, books of chronicles, as well as of law, arithmetic, philosophy and other departments of learning. Patrick Quhytlaw of New Grange, dying in 1607, left " twa gret kistis full of buikis of theologie, of the laws, physick, and utheris, to the number of v c. buikis "—a very considerable library for the time. David Wedderburn, the Dundee merchant, had a considerable collection, from which he used to lend freely to his friends and customers. To a neighbouring laird's son he lends " *Metamor-*

phosis Ovidii in Laten with the pictouris, bund in ane swynis skin of werry braw binding . . . for the space of ane moneth." His *Blundevill Drackis Voyages* was in great request, and another volume described as " my buik of walking sprittis " seems to have attracted curious enquirers.

The taste for voyages and " Buikis of the Sie " was characteristic of the time, for the advances in astronomy and navigation which followed from the Renaissance, and from such events as Columbus' discovery of the " new fund Yle," as a contemporary Scottish poet calls America, had led to a romantic interest in geographical knowledge. For the same reason it is not unusual to find a " Mappamounde," or map of the world, used as a piece of decoration in the rooms of the period. In the " Chalmer of the Foir Werk " at Cauldar there was one of these described as " ane brodit cart contenynge all cuntras," and such maps, whether printed or worked with the needle, were sometimes even hung in the place of honour " abune the burde." Paintings cannot be said to have come into general vogue in Scottish houses, but here and there enthusiasts were buying pictures abroad and helping to spread the taste for pictorial art in Scotland. One of these pioneers was Wedder-burn of Dundee, already mentioned, who used to arrange with friends going abroad to bring him back pictures from France or Flanders. John Barclay of Edinburgh, left " thrie paintit brodis with stories," and a year or two later one Erasmus Durie left as many as " seavin pictouris." The time was drawing near when the taste for pictures was to be much more widely diffused, and when George Jamesone was to set a high standard for Scottish portrait painters.

The sister art of music had also its devotees in Scotland. Even by the beginning of the sixteenth century we have records of the use of the harp, the fiddle, the lute, the organis,[1] the monocord, the taubron, the clarescha, the drone and the schalmis—an instrument of the clarinet type. Some verses written on the arrival of Anne of Denmark, nearly a century later, speak also of the regals, hautboy, virginals, gitterns, trumpets, timbrels, seistar sumphion, pipe and clarion. No doubt the pre-Reformation Church had done a good deal in spreading a taste for music and in providing a class of trained musicians. Writing of his student days in St. Andrews, which ended in 1574, James Melvill says, " I lerned my musicke of ane Alexander Smithe, servant to the Primarius of our Collage, wha had been treaned upe amangis the mounkis in the Abbay. I lerned of him the gam (gamut or scale), pleane-song and mony of the treables of the Psalmes. . . . I lovit singing and playing on instrumentis passing weill and

---

[1] See Plate XI.

wad gladlie spend tyme whar the exerceise thairof was within the Collage ; for twa or thrie of our condisciples played fellon weil on the virginals, and an uther on the lute and githorn. Our Regent also had the pinalds in his chalmer, and lernit something, and I eftir him." It is hard to say what the " pinalds " were, unless the word is a form of " spinet." In Italy the spinet dates from 1503, but the name " virginalls " was used in England for all such keyboard instruments for long after this, and the earliest reference to a spinet quoted in the *New English Dictionary* is from Pepys' *Diary* in 1664. Melville's reference goes back to a date ninety years earlier than this, though it was not written till about 1600. Still, it is difficult to see what distinction was intended between " virginalls " and " spinet." John Florio, in his *New Worlde of Wordes* gives a " paire of virginalles " as equivalent to the Italian " spinetta." Another instrument of the same kind was the clavichord, whose tone, however, was produced by a tangent instead of by the plucking of a quill. These keyboard instruments are seldom found in the inventories of Scottish houses of this period, yet we know that there was a good deal of domestic music. In Glasgow, for instance, before the Union of the Crowns, there was a musical coterie, for a contemporary diarist tells us of " a gentillman's

"PAIRE OF ORGANIS" (FIFTEENTH CENTURY) FROM TRIPTYCH BY
VAN DER GOES AT HOLYROOD PALACE
Copyright of His Majesty the King

house in the town wha enterteined maist expert singars and playars, and brought upe all his berns thairin." And no doubt there were similar groups of musical people elsewhere, and especially perhaps in the cathedral towns, where the musical tradition still lingered.

Returning from this musical digression to the furnishing of the sitting-rooms of the period, we may note that clocks were not yet in common use, and the hour-glass still stood on many a chimneypiece. There too might sometimes be found " ane boyst of tubacco," for, in spite of King James's prejudices, the practice of smoking was steadily gaining ground ; and the tinder match-box no doubt lay conveniently to hand. In the window there might be a wire cage containing a laverock, and among the odds and ends that lay about the room were such things as inkhorns and penners, a board and men for chess and backgammon, and materials for ladies' work. In the bedrooms we should find brushes and combs, sponges and shoe-horns, while warming-pans were in use for warming the beds.

How did life pass in these days ? The gentlemen of leisure had such sports as golf, catchpole, archery, hawking and coursing to amuse them, and golf balls, as well as many other requisites used in games of the period, were imported from Flanders. The following contemporary

advice given to " Gentillmen " gives an idea of
their preoccupations and responsibilities ·

First, in the mornyng, get vp with gud intent ;
To do your God seruice be ye diligent ;
To go to preiching ye do your bissy ceure,
Syne to your sport ye pass with avanteur ;
Exclude surfatt and spend with discretioun,
And luve your servand of gud condition ;
Lak not your kin, suppois thair wit be rude,
But help your freind in to his quarrell guid.

His wife is to be " cherreissit weill," and,
subject to her satisfactory behaviour, loved as
his own life. A sharp distinction is called for
in the treatment of sons and of daughters :

Teiche weill your sons, and gif him your counsale ;
Bot hald your dochter ay in stret bensale (control).

Finally, the gentleman is to " pay the seruand
his fie for his labour," and to " mak an leill man
his executeur," to keep patience under trials
till God send remeid, and to make " Schir
Ewstace," the uncomplaining huntsman saint,
his pattern and example.

As to the life of women, when a lady of
fashion awoke in the morning she found her
fire already burning brightly, and as soon as she
was ready to rise her maidens brought her her
slippers and her wyliecoat, comfortably warmed
for her use. Placing a velvet stool for her near
the fire, two of the maidens combed her hair
while she held her steel glass in her hand and

superintended their labours. When she was
fully dressed she drank a cup of Malvoisie,
sweetened with sugar, and then passed out into
the garden for a breath of fresh air, and ordered
her page to prepare her " disjune," or *déjeuner*,
consisting perhaps of a freshly roasted pair of
plovers, a partridge and a quail, with a cup of
sack. The next duty is to order the day's
dinner ; and this done she goes to inspect her
maidservants at their work, some of them
employed in making quoifs, ruffs and other fine
linen for her own use ; and of all such work
she is a severe and exacting critic, scolding the
maidens unmercifully if their work falls short
of her standard. Pleasantly fatigued with her
exertions, she withdraws to her chamber, for it
is now past noon, and refreshes herself with
whatever meat she has ordered and drinks a
cup or two of Muscadel, finishing off the repast
with some raisins or capers. The afternoon has
now to be passed till supper-time, and she may
either sit in the garden, or, if the day is cold, fall
asleep over a book at the fire. Supper is the
meal of the day, and as the meal proceeds
musicians enter and stimulate digestion by
playing on the organs, the lute and viol and
shalm and timbrel. Then comes an evening
stroll in the garden, after which her ladyship
retires to her chamber and sits gossiping so long
with her maidens that a final light collation is

required, with a draught of Rhenish wine, to fortify her for the hours of sleep.

Sometimes, of course, she leaves her house and garden and visits the tailor or the jeweller. Dressed in a rich and splendid robe, with double garnishings of gold, and her hair surmounted with crape, she is decked by her maidens with a velvet hat and her hood of state, and a mask is added to shield her complexion. A great gold chain is hung round her neck, with a necklace and half-chains of Paris work of exceptional fineness ; and her shoes are of velvet, over silk stockings. At the tailor's she discusses the last new " guise " or fashion—whether her new gown is to be made full, with many plaits and folds, or whether it is to fit more closely to the figure ; and there is the question of colour and materials, and she spends delightful hours comparing and examining plain and figured velvets, silks, satins, damask and grograin. There is plenty of room for fancy and fine taste ; for effects are got by cutting out a cloth over a material of different colour, and success in this pasmenting, or *appliqué* work, calls for both natural instinct and artistic imagination ; and as Madam handles the rich stuffs, savouring the texture between her heavily jewelled fingers, and from time to time drawing back the gold bracelets which keep slipping over her wrists, her brain is ever at work conceiving combina-

tions of colour and material, rejecting effects
unsuitable to her own style and figure, and
arriving at ideas which the tailor will have
to express in beautiful and becoming
costume.

Such a picture as I have given of the life of
the idle rich at the close of the sixteenth century
—a picture which is borrowed in every detail
from contemporary notes—must seem one of
gross self-indulgence. The eating and drinking
appears indecent to those who have tightened
their belts under the chastening compulsion of
the Food Controller. And, indeed, contemporary
writers tell us that in those days surfeit killed
more than sword and knife, and the medical
counsels of the time were largely directed
against the perils of over-eating. Sometimes
these counsels merely give blunt expression to
familiar, if inglorious, experience :

> Quha wald tak rest upoun the nicht,
> The supper sowld be schort and licht ;
> The stommok hes ane full grit pane
> Quhen at the supper mekle is tane.

Drinks that have gone flat are to be avoided, as
also are mixed meats. The various ways of
cooking meat are discussed ; " bulyeit " or
boiled meat, we are told, " fosteris weill " ;
" rostit " meat is said to dry the blood ; of salt
meat there is never a good word to say ; it is

pronounced " warst of ony fude," and we are
warned that it

> dois grit oppressioun
> To feble stomokis that nan nocht refrane ;
> For thingis contrair to thyne complexioun
> Off gredy throttis the stomokis has grit pane.

Much of the advice is sound. One is not to
eat till the previous meal has been " weill
degest " ; that nourishes best which savours
best ; " cleir air and walking makis gud deges-
tioun," and we are to beware of excess and of
" nodding heidis and of candill licht," or, in
other words, late hours. Other counsels are
more arbitrary. We are to comb our hair in the
morning, but " at evin I the forbid," no reason
being given. Sleeping at noon is forbidden,
for of that " cumis grit sweirnes " or disinclina-
tion for work ; and we are not at any time to
sleep on our back, which will hasten us to a
sudden death. To " couer weill thy heid " is
advised for health of body ; and to protect us
from " mistis blak, and air of pestilence " we
are to have a fire in the morning and a covered
bed, meaning, perhaps, a closely curtained bed,
at eve. On the whole the advice given is
founded on a sense of the importance of self-
control and moderation :

Qubair thyn awin gouernance may hald thyn hele (health).
Preiss neuir with medicinaris for to dele.

As to children's life in those early days, they were never at a loss for toys, for the best were those they devised for their own use. In mediæval illustrations we see children sailing little boats, running with paper windmills at the end of a stick, and amusing themselves in all kinds of simple ways. In James VI's time the development of a more intimate family life brought with it a new attention by grown-up people to the natural tastes of the young, and parents had new opportunities of knowing their children and taking pleasure in their company. Among the imports of the time we find children's dolls, under the name of " babeis," besides rattles and whistles, by which the overflowing energy of youth could be agreeably expressed in ear-splitting noise. If history is sometimes dull, surely it is because we hear so little of children in it, and the toys and lesson books and baby coats and shoes of a bygone age have a magical gift in humanising history and putting us in kindlier touch with the past. How vividly we feel the reality of Queen Mary's time when we read of a little boy who, as he sat by the sea by Montrose links, had two reasons for being specially happy. One was that his penknife had just been polished and sharpened by a cutler who had new come to the town ; and the other was that he had that morning bought a " pennie-worthe of aples." What could be more thrilling than to cut thin shavings from an apple with the newly sharpened knife ? As he was putting one of these shavings in his mouth, some sound attracted his attention and he began to " lope upe upon a little sandie bray " ; and, the loose sand slipping beneath his feet, he fell, and the knife, just missing his stomach, pierced his left knee to the bone ; " wherby," says this son of the Reformation, who had shortly before injured a schoolfellow " in the schin of the lag " with the same knife, " wherby the aequitie of God's judgment and my conscience struck me sa, that I was the mair war of knyffes all my dayes l "

Letters written in the early years of the seventeenth century throw occasional flashes of light on the relations between parents and children, and as we read we realise that, if there was more ceremony between the young and their elders than is the fashion of our day, there were the same natural affections, and also the same recurring problems as those which mark family life in our own time. Children, it appears, had even then an exasperating habit of outgrowing their clothes. And though the mothers often took an indulgent view of this symptom of healthy growth and would not have been unwilling to see their darlings in new and becoming apparel, the fathers were of sterner stuff, refused to admit that their children were going about like frights, thought that the old clothes might very well do for a bit yet, and, in fact, used every art to evade an uncongenial subject. We can sympathise with the Laird of Glenfalloch who, being off on his travels with his lady in 1619, and having left his two sons at Haddington in charge of a tutor, received a letter in which flattering reports on the boys' educational progress were ingeniously combined with the most unsparing condemnation of their wardrobe. " Send alsmekle cloth as will be ane gown to Jhone, and his ald gown wald serue for ane gown to Duncane. Jhone will be ane schollar, God willing, if he be nocht interrupted. Duncane begins weill, God saiff him. Assure the lady your wiffe that I sall haiff ane special cair under God of her sonnes that ar heir, and requeist her nocht to think long eftir thame. The dowblet ye caust mak to Duncane is now up at the slot of his breist. Ye wald say that he wearis his belt as men sayis Mr. George Buchanan did weare his, the dowblet is growen so schort." After some reflections on ecclesiastical affairs the tutor concludes his letter, " God His mercy be with you, and restis your awin, efter the ald maner, Mr. William Bowie." And then, knowing his laird, and foreseeing that his remarks on church politics and his pious aspirations may be made use of to banish the memory of more pressing and practical questions, he returns to the charge in one peremptory post-script—"*Duncane mon haiff an vther dow-blett.*"

LECTURE V

THE KING OR THE COVENANT

CHARLES I, 1625-1649

The Covenanting Period—Ascetic views of life—A Covenanter's courtship, with an eighteenth-century contrast—Conditions unfavourable to the development of furniture—New Scottish industries—Furniture and fashions from London—A Scottish nobleman's house—" The laiche hall "—The dining-room and silver plate—The drawing-room—New ideas in furniture and ornaments—The lettermeitt house—Bedrooms—Development of beds in Scotland—The knop sek—The strek bed—The leta-camp bed—Kaissit beds—The box-ped or buistie—The " laych-rynnand " or truckle bed—The laird's mistake—The four-poster—Royal beds—Devices on the Queen of Scots' bed—Mourning beds and mourning customs—Queen Mary's bed-curtains from Loch Leven—Heraldic decoration of beds—Changing fashions in colours and colour names.

OUR survey of the development of domestic life in Scotland now brings us to the Covenanting period, when the ecclesiastical differences which had manifested themselves under James VI became more acute, and the national preference for a Presbyterian system of church government brought the people into direct conflict with the throne and began to loosen their tenacious loyalty to the House of Stuart. By his marriage with the Catholic princess, Henrietta Maria, Charles I forfeited the confidence of Presbyterian Scotland and exposed himself to much jealous and suspicious misunderstanding of his conduct and motives. It was his misfortune that his high conception of his duties and prerogatives as King was not tempered by something of the watchful caution of his father, and something of his father's instinct for studying men and waiting for the opportune moment. Thus the Act of Revocation—involving most of the property of the pre-Reformation Church, which had been distributed by James.VI among the nobles—drove the nobility to the Presbyterian side, undoing at a blow what it had cost James much labour and ingenuity to accomplish. The imposition of Laud's *Service Book* by authority of King Charles immediately called forth the National league and Covenant, a protest which was enthusiastically signed. A year later Sir Edward Verney, writing home from the English army encamped near Berwick, said, " Wee find all the meaner sort of men uppon the Scotch Border well inclyned to the King . . . but the Gentlemen are all Covenanters."

As soon, however, as the pacification of Berwick had reinstated Presbyterianism, the Scottish clergy made the signature of the National Covenant compulsory, thus arrogating to themselves the right to dictate the national religion—the very right which they had denied to the King. It was not long before the nobles began to realise how little their alliance with the Presbyterian ministers was based on any real harmony of view or congeniality of feeling. It was against all their traditions to submit to the domination of men whose origin and upbringing inclined them to look with disfavour on habits, recreations and indeed the whole scale of social amenity to which the upper classes had always been accustomed ; and it galled them to be dictated to by ministers on whom they looked down as social inferiors. The result was a revulsion against the system set up by the Covenant and an inevitable reaction of Royalist sympathies, and the country was split into two camps—a division which really arose not from mere class feeling, but from the opposition of two irreconcilable views of life. For the student of the domestic arts the evidences of this divergence of view are too plain to be passed by.

Much as Scotland owes to the Covenanters, for their contribution to Scottish mind and character can hardly be overestimated, the religion which animated them was of a singularly austere and forbidding type. Scores of contemporary diaries have familiarised us with its solitary and introspective character. It was the fashion of the time to keep a minute record of the individual's religious experiences, in

which were detailed the clouds of doubt and
distrust, the entanglements of temptation and
spiritual " discurradgement," the covenants
made, broken and renewed, the darknesses and
self-abhorrences, and the occasional clearnesses,
often resulting from the sudden recollection of
some appropriate scriptural text from which
the struggling soul " gott some sweete and
comfortabl discoverie " of grace ; and then the
frequent reaction, when " Satan began to
whisper in my minde, oh I fear this will be lyke
the morning cloud and the earlie dew, that
soon passeth away." Even a schoolboy, having
been " intised " into playing games upon the
" saboth day," writes, " I fell into such dread-
full terrors that was insupportabl, aprehending
it could not consist with the justice of God but
that the earth should open and swallow me up
to hell qwick." It was an unhappy consequence
of the current interpretation of the doctrine of
salvation by faith and not by works, that attention was focussed on states or " frames " of
mind, as if these were in themselves more
important than the faithful performance of the
allotted task.

To men of this mould every natural impulse
was apt to appear as a snare of the devil, and
every event of life as merely a phase of the
conflict with Apollyon. Even love-making was
no idyllic interlude. Mr. John Livingstone in

his *Memoirs* tells us how a marriage was " propounded " to him by a third party with the daughter of an Edinburgh merchant. Propounded ! The very word might dissipate the rosiest of dreams ! " I had seen her before several times," he says, " and had heard the testimony of many of her gracious disposition, yet I was for nine months seeking, as I could, direction from God about that business ; during which time I did not offer to speak to her, who, I believe, had not heard anything of the matter, only for want of clearness in my mind, although I was twice or thrice in the house, and saw her frequently at communions and public meetings ; and it is like I might have been longer in such darkness except the Lord had presented me an occasion of our conferring together ; for in November, 1634, when I was going to the Friday meeting at Ancrum, I met with her and some others going thither, and propounded to them by the way to confer upon a text whereupon I was to preach the day after at Ancrum ; wherein I found her conference so judicious and spiritual that I took that for some answer to my prayer to have my mind cleared, and blamed myself that I had not before taken occasion to confer with her. Four or five weeks later I propounded the matter to her and desired her to think upon it, and after a week or two I went to her mother's house, and being alone with her, desiring her answer, I went to prayer, and urged her to pray, which at last she did ; and in that time I got abundance of clearness that it was the Lord's mind that I should marry her, and then propounded the matter more fully to her mother. And although I was fully cleared, I may truly say it was above a month before I got marriage affection to her, although she was for personal endowment beyond many of her equals ; and I got it not till I had obtained it by prayer. But thereafter I had a great difficulty to moderate it."

This is one way of love. Let us not judge too harshly the pious procrastinations of our Covenanting Romeo. The course of true love never did run smooth. And the story of Mr. Livingstone's courtship, with its reluctant advances, its palsied intermissions, and its triumphant and indeed somewhat unbridled close, serves to remind us once more that " stony limits cannot hold love out." Keeping before our eyes the romantic picture of the two on their evening walk to Ancrum, and overhearing in fancy their Doric accents raised in exegetic heat over the disembowelment of some knotty text—culled, it may be, from the book of Habakkuk—let us be content to murmur with the poet :

How silver sweet sound lovers' tongues by night,
Like softest music to attendant ears !

And now, by way of emphasising Mr Livingstone's psychology by contrast, and because it is well to study the spirit of one century in its development or reaction in the next, let us compare his narrative with an eighteenth-century letter from a lady whose affections have been touched. " Mr. Shapely," she writes, " is the prettiest gentleman about town. He is very tall, but not too tall neither. He dances like an angel. His mouth is made, I do not know how, but it is the prettiest that I ever saw in my life. He is always laughing, for he has an infinite deal of wit. If you did but see how he rolls his stockings ! He has a thousand pretty fancies, and I am sure, if you saw him, you would like him. He is a very good scholar, and can talk Latin as fast as English. I wish you could but see him dance ! Now you must understand poor Mr. Shapely has no estate ; but how can he help that, you know ? And yet my friends are so unreasonable as to be always teasing me about him because he has no estate. . . . I forgot to tell you that he has black eyes, and looks upon me now and then as if he had tears in them. And yet my friends are so unreasonable, that they would have me be uncivil to him ! I have a good por- tion which they cannot hinder me of . . . but everyone here is Mr. Shapely's enemy. I desire therefore you will give me your advice, for

I know you are a wise man ; and if you advise
me well, I am resolved to follow it. I heartily
wish you could see him dance, and am, Sir,
Your most humble servant, B. D."

This is another way of love. You will admit
that in these two instances the mating instinct
operates somewhat diversely, so that one could
hardly have suspected that the seventeenth-
century minister and the eighteenth-century
belle were passing through the same crisis of the
affections. Each, perhaps, might with advantage have learned something of the other. Had
the young lady propounded to Mr. Shapely to
confer upon a portion of scripture, with a view
to ascertaining whether his conference was
judicious and spiritual, she might have discovered that that was not the kind of portion
that most appealed to him. And had Mr.
John Livingstone, without the long months of
painful propoundings, admitted into his lugu-
brious bosom so much natural marriage affection for the lady as to write, " Her mouth is
made, I do not know how, but it is the prettiest
that I ever saw in my life," I do not think that
either God or man would have laid it too
heavily to his charge.

But I quote Mr. Livingstone's romance, and
contrast it with the engaging foolishness of the
later specimen, because it exemplifies an attitude
of mind that was common in Scotland and else-

where in the seventeenth century. Mr. Livingstone represents a generation to whom anything
beyond an elementary standard of domestic
comfort was luxury and self-indulgence, and
any regard for beauty and ornament was a
concession to the lust of the eye and the pride
of life. Where such views are held we need not
look for any development of the artistic aspect
of household life. Like the pilgrims in Bunyan's
allegory, the Covenanters " set very light by all
the wares of the merchandisers ; they cared not
so much as to look upon them ; and if any
called upon them to buy, they would put their
fingers in their ears and cry, ' Turn away mine
eyes from beholding vanity.' "

The Puritan spirit, however, was not the
only cause which operated against any general
diffusion of luxury in domestic furnishing.
In 1628 Scotland was bankrupt. The nobles,
thanks to the Act of Revocation, had their own
troubles. Among the merchants and tradesmen
there were many whose enterprise and industry
had amassed considerable fortunes, but Charles'
repeated attempts at legislation against usury
made it difficult for such men to invest their
means profitably, and thus deprived Scottish
trade of the capital necessary to its expansion.
Yet progress was by no means arrested. As
family life developed, new wants began to discover themselves ; and this and the introduction

of new materials and industries brought about changes which, though small in themselves, had a gradual and cumulative effect in enriching the setting of domestic life.

About 1620, for instance, English tanners were brought into Scotland to instruct the native tanners in " the true and perfect form of tanning." Leather, accordingly, in spite of the imposition of a special tax, came into increased use for all sorts of domestic purposes. The inventory of an Edinburgh wright burgess, who died a few years later, includes a considerable stock of leather backs for chairs, and of red skins destined no doubt for the same purpose. At Rusco Tower Lady Lochinvar had " six gilt ledder cuscheounes " ; and leather was also used for the cases in which knives and spoons, brushes and combs, and many other household goods were enclosed.

Another industry which took root in Scotland at the same time was glass making. A small glass works was set going by Sir George Hay in the village of Wemyss, and after some ups and downs the venture proved successful. A Commission appointed by the Privy Council examined the glass and reported that it was fully as good as Danskine glass, though its thickness and toughness still left something to be desired. A conditional protection against foreign competition was accordingly granted, and to prevent the native manufacturer from taking unfair advantage of his monopoly a maximum price for " braid glas," meaning sheet glass, was fixed at twelve pounds the cradle. Glass had of course been in use in Scotland long before this. St. Margaret's Chapel, in Edinburgh Castle, had glass windows in 1336; and, among secular buildings, the palaces of Linlithgow and Falkland had their windows glazed in the year 1505. By the time with which we are now dealing every small town had its " glasenwricht " or glazier. As to glass vessels James IV had a cupboard of these in 1503, and as we have seen, foreign-made bottles and drinking-glasses had come into fashion in James VI's time. But it is only after the setting up of the glass works at Wemyss that we find table glass in common use in ordinary houses, different shapes being made for wine, beer and other beverages. Foreign glass of course also remained in use, and Lord Melville had a cupboard of Venice glass valued at five hundred pounds.

Along with glass we may note the gradual introduction of earthenware dishes, though whether these were of native manufacture is not clear. In most houses tin or pewter dishes continued to be used, while here and there the earlier " tree " or wooden dishes were still employed. Earthenware dishes had been im-

10

ported from Holland by Halyburton in the fifteenth century, but it is not till Charles I's reign that we find frequent reference to their domestic use. Though subject to breakage they had the advantage of being cheaper and more easily kept clean than pewter, and as they are sometimes described as painted their colour decoration may have been an additional attraction.

Earthenware was also used for less utilitarian purposes. The tradition which furnishes the cottage chimney-piece with highly glazed and boldly coloured dogs or human figures is an ancient one. In 1562 there was among the effects of Queen Mary " ane figure of ane doig " made in white earthenware, and such figures are often found in Charles I's time. It is startling at first sight to read that Mr. John Bonyman, dying in 1631, left among other things " thrie lame babies and three lame doges," but the notion that his house offered hospitality to cripples of all descriptions may be dismissed. These " babies " were merely small figures which, like the dogs, were made of " lame," that is loam or earthenware.

Another influence which must be taken into account as contributing to progress in house furnishing was the increasing familiarity with English standards of comfort and elegance. It had become customary for the well-to-do to send to London for their furniture. Thus on his daughter's engagement to Lord Cardross, Sir Thomas Hope, the Lord Advocate, who was an open supporter of the Covenant, made a " nott of some furnischings to be coft in London and sent home." He estimated the cost at two hundred pounds sterling, and added, " With Godis grace I sal sie the samyn thankfullie payit." The so-called furnishings included some " abillzeamentis " for the bride, for fashions in dress were also set in London. Many a gentlewoman in Scotland, profoundly distrusting local standards of fashion, must have had recourse to agonised appeals such as that addressed by one of their English provincial sisters to a friend in London—" I pray send me word if wee bottone petticotes and wastcotes wheare they most be Botend."

That we may have an idea of the actual arrangements and furnishing of the time, let us examine some of the principal rooms of the house of a Scottish nobleman who died in 1643. The house may be taken as fairly typical of its class, and it is interesting because it illustrates the transition from the lingering mediæval tradition to a still immature appreciation of the possibilities of family, as contrasted with feudal, life.

Of the kitchen we need only remark that it is on the ground floor, that it is well supplied with brazen pots and pans and cooking utensils of all kinds, and that there are many dozen of tin plates, all of which are engraved with the family arms. No seats of any kind are provided for the servants' use.

We may also pass by the " Gentlemen's chalmer," only remarking, as to the significance of the name, that as one writer puts it " our nobility must needs have their menials gentle-manised," and that the room was occupied by menservants, some of whom slept in beds and others on shake-downs on the floor. The application of the word " gentleman " to men-servants is not an exclusively Scottish use ; but the English traveller, Christopher Lowther, was struck in 1629 by the fact that Scottish gentlefolk called their men and maids Misters and Mistresses. Probably the Scottish tendency to greater formality in forms of address is one of the traces of early association with France.

The special interest of the house begins with the " Laiche Hall." In the mediæval house, as we have seen, the hall was the principal apart-ment, and it was always on the first floor. But now that the family had withdrawn from the hall to the private Dining-room and Drawing-room, the hall lost its importance and was relegated by the architects of the time to the ground floor, which was associated by tradition with the cellars and vaults, while the first floor was reserved for the more modern sitting-rooms used by the family. The Laiche Hall, thus banished, still bears some resemblance to the feudal hall of earlier days. Its walls are covered with hangings, it is furnished with an extending table surrounded by chairs in place of the older-fashioned board and forms, and there is a large fireplace in which a hospitable fire might still blaze. But the hangings are worth comparatively little, the fine arras being reserved for the rooms upstairs ; the chairs are only five in number, showing how little company the old hall sees in its declining days ; and the fireplace is unfurnished save for a pair of tongs. In a word, the hall has outlived its purpose and is already half-way towards the cheerless no man's land that it has become in the modern house.

Above the hall is the modern room which has supplanted it—the " Dyneing Room." Here are displayed seven pieces of arras hangings, clothing the walls with rich colour. Instead of the mediæval board there are five Spanish tables, besides three others kept in reserve in another part of the house. These were probably of uniform size so that any number required might be set in contact to form one continuous table, either straight or with rectangular extensions. In the room itself there are seats for as many as twenty-two guests, and this number could of course be supplemented if necessary. All of these seats were covered with " carpet," a thick woollen material. Ten of them, having backs, were used for the more important guests, while the remainder were stools or tabourets. The windows had striped hangings ; there was a long Persian carpet valued at five hundred merks, and three short carpets which may have been used as table-covers. At the fireside, which was furnished with shovel and tongs, stood two vessels for holding coal. These were made of tin and were valued at one hundred merks.

It will be noticed that neither in the hall nor in the dining-room is there a cupboard or dresser, nor any form of buffet or serving-table. Yet in the pantry we shall find that the silver for the table is what might be looked for in a house of this character. There are two silver basins and ewers, each set weighing 12 lb. and one of the sets being gilt ; two great gilt and chiselled silver cups with covers ; tankards and tumblers of silver ; a great silver salt-fatt ; two large silver candlesticks, two dozen silver spoons, and twelve silver dessert dishes. There is no mention of forks except that there is a case containing eleven knives followed by an entry of " ane fork." The fact that the fork was a single one shows that it was used only for serving fruit or some such special purpose.

The tumblers mentioned in this list were tumblers in the literal and original sense of the word, for having no flat base they would not stand upright on the table, but had to be emptied and turned upside down. They are spoken of by Samuel Pepys some twenty years later, and his reference to them is the earliest known to the *New English Dictionary*.

After the dining-room, and probably communicating with it, comes the drawing-room, one of the earliest instances in Scotland of a room called by that name. We are so familiar with the social uses of the drawing-room in our own day that we can hardly realise the vagueness with which people in the first half of the seventeenth century were feeling for a type of room which should answer the scarcely defined wants of their social life. There was no precedent, no tradition to give them a lead. The room was one to withdraw to after supper, and in it the dessert was no doubt eaten ; but what were the occupations or amusements with a view to which the room was to be furnished ? In the mediæval hall there had been musicians and sometimes visits from jugglers and other wandering performers. These, however, belonged to an age that was past, and the family, thrown on its own resources, had to devise its own methods of passing the time. In many households this would present no difficulty, but there are also people who have little initiative in such matters and who find themselves at a loss unless they are entertained by others. The house under our notice shows little evidence of any organised family life. The drawing-room was a room with a fireplace and two turrets. In each of these turrets, or " studies," as they are called, there was a carpet stool ; in the drawing-room itself there were only a set of eight chairs with padded backs, covered with blue and red satin damask, and a reposing chair " conforme," or *en suite*. There is no table of any kind, though sometimes, perhaps, some of the Spanish tables in the dining-room may be brought in ; no cabinets or aumries ; no musical instruments nor signs of chess, backgammon or cards ; no curtains, blinds nor carpet ; still less are there books, or pictures, or bowls for flowers, or a clock. Besides the handsome set of chairs and couch there is nothing of any kind whatever save a shovel and tongs by the fireside, and one other article so strangely out of keeping with modern ideas of a drawing-room that it must not be ignored—a chamber pot.

From the absence of comfortable furnishings we see that while the drawing-room had been adopted as a new and fashionable addition to the family apartments, many a Scottish family had some difficulty in adapting its habits to the use of such a room. In the house we are examining "My Lordis bed chamber" was supplied with a "wrytting standard," and he no doubt preferred to write his letters there. And it is probable that the comparative novelty of private bedrooms—each with its separate entrance, instead of opening off one another— through which other persons did not keep coming and going on their way to their own rooms, tempted inmates of the house to neglect the new public rooms and the social life that ought to have united the family there.

Of course ideas of furnishing and standards of comfort varied very widely even in houses of the same class. Lord Stormonth, for instance, who died in 1636, had in his house many of the things we have missed in the cheerless and scantily furnished drawing-room that has been described. Not only had he portraits on the walls, but he cultivated music, for there was a pair of organs ; and we find also needlework chairs and embroideries, and chess and back-gammon boards. In which room these were kept, however, we are not told, so we can draw no inference as to the development of a particular type of room corresponding to the modern drawing-room.

But however the contents of Scottish houses were distributed over the various rooms—and early inventories seldom give this information

—there was a distinct advance in the richness
and variety of furnishing and ornaments.   In
addition to the Turkey and Persian carpets
that have already been mentioned we learn
that China carpets were also known ; and as
showing the wide geographical range from
which the wants of Scottish homes were supplied, one house in Aberdeen had Dutch table-
cloths, Venice sponges, Indian saucers, Musco-
vite goblets and Turkish turbans ! This may
be an exceptional instance, due perhaps to some
member of the household having followed the
sea ; but foreign ornaments and curiosities were
by no means uncommon, one favourite ornament being what were called " Indana noot-
scheillis "—in other words, coco-nuts, set on a
silver stem and lined, or at least lipped, with
silver.

Among the changes which followed from the
abandonment of the hall and the separation of
the life of the family from that of the servants,
was the introduction of the domestic handbell,
which now became necessary to summon the
servants when they were wanted. It was not
till the opening years of the eighteenth century
that it was superseded by the bell hung in the
kitchen and rung by wires from the various
rooms. Another sign of the times was the
introduction of the basin-stand. It was at
first used only in the hall or dining-room, in

whichever a particular family might dine, and it went by the name of the " knaiff " or knave. A young lad had hitherto held the basin in which the principal persons washed their hands before a meal, but the new tendencies led to his place being taken by a wooden " standard " or stand, which was accordingly called after him on the same principle as that on which we call a revolving table with two or three stages a " dumb waiter," or on which a fireside candlestick is called a " carle " or a " peerman " in various parts of Scotland. These alterations in the domestic arrangements also gave rise to a new apartment in the architecture of the time, known as the " lettermeitt house." It was in effect a mess-room for men-at-arms or an upper servants' hall, and it derived its name from the fact that the joints at the family meals were removed when done with and served at the later-meat house. Inventories show that the linen for the lettermeitt house was intermediate in quality between the linen used by the family and that thought good enough for the kitchen.

The bedrooms of the time showed a considerable advance on the days when there was often little furniture beyond the bed or beds, a chest, and sometimes a table and form or stool ; yet they lacked many things which we now count elementary necessities. The swinging toilet mirror not yet having been introduced, the dressing-table as we know it did not exist, though in France a draped table with brushes and shaving materials is shown in one of Abraham Bosse's engravings, and a framed mirror was often, no doubt, propped up on a table by the window. More often they were hung upon the wall, or only a hand-glass was used. Such as they were these mirrors no doubt served the same purpose that ours do to-day—to gratify a woman's longing to see that everything is right, and relieve a man's anxiety to see that nothing is wrong. Nothing like the modern commodious wardrobe was to be found, and the clothes were still kept in a chest, in the lower part of which, however, were now sometimes fitted a couple of " shuttles " or drawers. Neither is there any washstand, and, indeed, if it was usual to wash in the bedroom at all, which it probably was not, a basin and ewer must have been brought for the purpose by a servant. Baths are never mentioned, and when these were taken it was in a large tub or " baith-fatt," with which, in mediæval days, a canopy had been used to ensure a measure of privacy. Public baths, which played so important a part in foreign town life in the fifteenth century, and which, it must be added, generally acquired so doubtful a reputation, do not seem to have existed in Scotland till early in the second half of the seventeenth century, when there were

" bath stoves " or " sweiting balnes " in Edinburgh.

But, to tell the plain truth, neither in Scotland nor elsewhere had habits of personal cleanliness yet come into fashion. It is probably true that, as M. Henri Havard suggests in his book, *L'art et le Confort*, the origin of the fashion which led ladies in the eighteenth century to receive visitors while they performed their toilette, was an ostentatious pride in the display of standards of cleanliness which were a reaction against the slovenly neglect that had hitherto prevailed. Washing, so far from being a habit, was only occasional, though, as we have seen, the hands were superficially cleansed at meals. A French writer on manners proposed what was no doubt considered a high standard when he urged his readers to take the trouble to wash their hands every day, and their faces " nearly as often "! He added that the head too should sometimes be washed. This was in Charles I's time, when men as well as women wore long hair, and the counsel was all the more necessary, if also all the more troublesome to carry out. It was, in fact, the increasing desire for cleanliness that eventually led to the adoption of the periwig.

Another advance in manners was the use of the handkerchief, which however was still by no means general. Handkerchiefs had been known

in the sixteenth century, but Erasmus enum-
crates various primitive and unseemly expe-
dients practised by his contemporaries in
attending to what we may delicately call nasal
hygiene, all of which were evidently more
usual than the use of the handkerchief. Another
writer some years later, giving rules for elegant
deportment in society, says that if in blowing
your nose you use a handkerchief " you will
earn great praise " ! One of Abraham Bosse's
engravings shows a seventeenth-century interior
in which a lady uses a handkerchief, and in
doing so she turns her head away from the
company—a rule of politeness dating from the
days when handkerchiefs were not in use.

The bedrooms, however, were pleasant enough
rooms. In ordinary houses the walls were
painted or whitewashed, the mean if convenient
practice of using wall-papers not having been
introduced till after 1800, when " China papers "
began to come into fashion. In more elegantly
furnished houses there would be hangings of
camlet or of arras, while occasionally, as in
Lady Melville's bedchamber at Monymaill,
the walls were hung with stamped and gilded
leather. The furniture generally consisted of
a chair and stools covered with stuff to match
the bed-curtains, and a table covered with the
same material. The whole suite thus made up
was considered as going with, and forming

part of the equipment of, the bed. Beyond the chest and mirror already mentioned and sometimes a shelved aumrie or press, there was little else but the candlesticks.

The principal piece of furniture was of course the bed itself, and it may be worth while to cast back and review the development of beds, and especially of some of the varieties that were characteristic of Scotland.

George Buchanan, writing of the hardy habits of the Highlanders, says, " In their houses also they lie upon the ground, strewing fern or heath upon the floor with the roots downward, and the leaves turned up." And he adds that they had the greatest contempt for pillows and blankets. In early times it was very much in this fashion that the retainers in Scottish castles passed the night in the hall, making themselves as comfortable as they could on straw or heather, or, as civilisation advanced, on sacks or rude mattresses filled with flock, and known as " knop seks." Before the end of the fifteenth century stand beds, which were beds raised from the floor on " stoups " or legs, were used by all the more important persons in the household. There were various forms of stand beds. The " strek " bed seems to have been one in which the mattress was laid on stretched supports instead of on boards. The " letacamp " or camp bed (*lit de camp*), sometimes amusingly perverted into " litigant," was originally a folding bed suitable for carrying on a journey, and we read in the Lord High Treasurer's Accounts for 1489 of " tursing (i.e. packing and transporting) the kingis letacamp bed to Dunbertane." Such beds were often fitted with a portable canopy, so that the traveller, even if the bed had to be set up for the night in squalid surroundings, might have his own seemly hangings round him. When a nobleman with his family and retinue went from one of his country seats to another, all the necessary furniture, including tapestries, beds, and sometimes even the windows and doors, was carried with them. When the Percy family in England travelled there was an order that one bed must serve for every two priests or gentlemen, and one for every three children. In Scottish houses the stand beds had a covering of serge, kersey or arras, and they were fitted with blankets and sheets as well as bolsters and pillows with the necessary " codware " or pillow covers. The use of a " rufe," or canopy, with curtains was very common, but it was suspended from the ceiling and did not form part of the bed. The four-poster, in which the canopy is supported on the posts, first appears in the list of beds belonging to James V in 1539. This is the most important type, and we shall return to it after describing some other varieties.

The introduction of " kaissit " beds, in which wooden boarding or panelling took the place of hanging drapery, is only a phase of the movement which brought panelled walls into fashion instead of tapestry. Among the " insicht geir " in Dumbarton Castle in 1580 was a " stand bed of eastland timmer with ruf and pannell of the same," the pannel, or pane, being the vertical part rising from behind the pillow to the back of the canopy. But thirty years earlier Laurence Murray, of Tullibardine, had left among his effects " twa clois beddis." These were the characteristic box beds, known also as " buisties " or " boushties," still to be found in many a cottage. Their use was noted by Fynes Moryson, the English traveller, who, being in Scotland " upon occasion of businesse " in 1598, thus described them : " Their bedsteads were then like Cubbards in the wall, with doors to be opened and shut at pleasure so as we climbed up to our beds. They use but one sheete, open at the sides and top, but close at the feete, and so doubled." The enclosing of the bed with wooden doors or sliding panels was the outcome of the contemporary desire for " close " rooms. Tapestried chambers were too often draughty and uncomfortable and our forefathers' ambition was to have their rooms air-tight so as to exclude draughts. The discomforts of closeness, in the modern sense of

exhausted and vitiated air, had still to be discovered, and the early box beds, which excluded
light and air, were no doubt considered in their
day the last word in luxury. Early in the seventeenth century Gordon, of Abergeldie, had " ane
clos kaissit bed, lokkit and bandit " in which
we may assume that he slept secure not only
from the intrusions of man, but also from the
insidious encroachments of ventilation. Such
beds were often provided with a bed-staff,
which Johnson's *Dictionary* erroneously defines
as " a pin to keep the clothes from slipping."
In *Satan's Invisible World Discovered* there is a
tale of a ghostly visitant in which this incident
is related : " The night after, it (the apparition)
came panting like a dog out of breath ; upon
which one took up a bed-staff to knock, which
was caught out of her hand and thrown away."
This is the only literary reference to the use of
the bed-staff which I know. No doubt the bed-
staff was so used to knock with when there were
no bells to call attendants, but its characteristic
use was in arranging the bedclothes on a bed
which was only accessible from one side—
spreading them smooth and tucking them in on
the further side. For this purpose it is still in
use in Fife and elsewhere.

Probably the " bureau " bed, used in the
eighteenth century, was a descendant of the
box bed. It was made to fold back during the

day on a hinge near the floor into a niche in the wall.

> The white-washed wall, the nicely sanded floor,
> The varnished clock that click'd behind the door ;
> The chest, contrived a double debt to pay,
> A bed by night, a chest of drawers by day.

So Goldsmith describes it, and in many houses designed by the brothers Adam it was used to economise space in the servants' quarters.

One other form of bed worth mentioning is the truckle bed. Truckle beds were employed at Magdalen College, Oxford, in 1459, but they seem only to have come into use in Scotland in the sixteenth century. A personal servant was thus enabled to sleep in his master's room on a bed which by day was run under the standing bed on which his master slept. In 1566 the " Wyide Chalmer," of Calder House, had " ane turnit bed with ane draw bed under of plane tre," while in another room there was what is described as " ane laych rynnand (low running) bed "—another name for the same thing. It was this arrangement, whereby the master slept on a higher level than his servant, which misled the Scottish Laird who, arriving at an English inn with his servant, was given a room with a four-poster. " Such furniture being new to the Highlanders "—I quote from an old chapbook —" they mistook the four-posted pavillion for the two beds, and the Laird mounted the tester while the man occupied the comfortable lodging below. Finding himself wretchedly cold in the night, the Laird called to Donald to know how he was accommodated. ' Ne'er sae weel a' my life,' quothe the ghilly. ' Ha, man,' exclaimed the Laird, ' if it wasna for the honour of the thing I could find it in my heart to come doun.' " Such pretentious furniture was not to be found in Scottish inns, where the accommodation was of the most primitive kind, and there was, as a Scottish traveller remarked on returning north of the Tweed, " a sensible decay of service by that a man has in England." But it must be borne in mind that the upper classes in Scotland did not make use of the inns, being usually able to count on the hospitality of persons of their own rank. The inns, therefore, laying themselves out for a lower class of visitor, did not make a favourable impression on travellers in Scotland. One complains that " the bottom of my bed was loose boards, one laid over another, and a thin bed upon it " ; while another speaks of " mean beds where we might have rested had the mice not randezvoused over our faces."

In private houses, however, the four-poster soon established itself, and the royal inventories show us that such beds were richly decorated and must have given an imposing air to the rooms in which they were placed. One of those belonging to James V was hung with purple velvet with fringes and tassels of silver ; others were draped in crimson or equally rich colours, while it was not unusual to employ " variant," or shot silk, whose play of colour must have produced effects of great splendour. Various kinds of decoration were made use of in ornamenting the royal beds. Some were " pasmentit," that is, enriched by the application of gold and silver lace, while needlework and embroidery were also employed. Thus another of James V's beds had a " rufe with ane heid and overfrontale of cramosy velvott, with the storie of the life of man upoune the samune, comparit to a hart, all in raisit wark in gold, silver and silk." In Queen Mary's time the royal beds were even more elaborate, and in their decoration embroidery and needlework were carried to a high pitch. One comparatively plain bed among them is of some historical interest. It is described as " of violett broun veluot, pasmentit with a pasment made of gold and silver, furnished with ruif, headpiece and pandis," and it had curtains of violet damask. It was in this bed, given by the Queen to Darnley in August, 1566, that Darnley was asleep in his lodging in the Kirk o' Field when the explosion took place which caused his death. So much violence and tragedy is covered by the terse note in the inventory " the said bed was tint in the Kingis ludgeing." Even what are inventoried as " plane beddis not enrichit with onything " were sometimes rather gay for modern standards of taste. One, for example, was " of veluot, reid yallow and blew " with " thrie curtenis of dames (damask) of the same cullouris unfreinyett " (unfringed)—as though the shy god of sleep were to be caught lurking in the rainbow !

Among the State Papers relating to Queen Mary is one (No. 408) dated October, 1587, giving a list of " Devices on the Queen of Scots Bed." About fifty of these allegorical devices are described. In the description of them there are several references to colour. It is possible, of course, that the devices may have been carved on the wood of the bed, and then heightened with colour and gilded. But it is much more probable, and quite in accordance with the usage of the time, that the so-called bed is really a bedcover, probably the same as that referred to in the inventory of articles left in possession of " Andrew Melvin, gent " (State Papers, No. 292), and there described as " Furniture for a bed, wroughte with needle woorke of silke, silver and gold, with divers devices and armes, not throughlie finished." Many of the devices and mottoes are philosophical reflections on the fateful circumstances of Mary's life. One represents " A Lioness and her little cub near to her " with the motto, " Unum quidem, sed leonem." Another shows " A dove in a cage, and an eagle above ready to devour her when she shall come forth," with the motto in Italian, " I am in evil plight, but I fear worse." A third consists of " Two crowns on earth and one in heaven, composed of stars with flames of fire issuing from them," and the motto, " Manet ultima cœlo."

One characteristic custom of the time was the use of mourning beds draped in black. The statement is constantly repeated that mourning was unknown in Scotland till the death of Queen Magdalen in 1537, the authority of George Buchanan having been accepted without question. So far as it applies to public mourning the statement may be correct. An order subscribed by the King was inserted in the books of the Edinburgh Town Council in July, 1537 (the date of the Queen's death), which, without express reference to that event, says, " The lords understandis that the Kingis grace and all the lieges of his realm hes instantly ado with blak veluott, satyne, dammes and all sorts of blak clayth . . ." and goes on to forbid raising the price. But private mourning was worn long before this. It is mentioned in Dunbar's poem of the " Wedow," which was in print by 1508. This lady describes how she goes to the kirk " cled in cairweeds," talks of her " dule habits," and tells us that her " clokkis thai are cairful (sorrowful) in colour of sable," and such allusions entitle us to assume that mourning was by that time a well-established custom. The bed which appears among the possessions of James V in 1542, and which was hung in black " dalmes " (damask), was probably so draped in sorrow for the death of his French bride. At any rate, it was not unusual, as the sixteenth century went on, for well-to-do families to have a special bed for use in times of mourning, or at least a complete set of black hangings. The same practice ruled in England. In the *Verney Memoirs* (Vol. I, p. 293) Sir Ralph Verney writes to a relative who has announced the death of her husband, and suggests lending her " the great black bed and hangings from Claydon " as the only consolation he can offer ; and it seems to have been customary to send this bed round to any branch of the family which had to go into mourning. In Queen Mary's inventories we find three such beds, two of velvet and one of damask, entirely in black, with black silk fringes. In 1594 the Laird of Caddalis had two of these funereal beds, draped in black velvet with black taffeta curtains ; and when we examine the wearing apparel in his house we find fresh evidence of a period of mourning. There are black velvet " cornettis," which are the well-known head-dresses shaped like two horns, worn by women ; three " blak mwchis

of talphetie " ; and, most unmistakable of all,
" ane braid craip for the duill." As time went
on our forefathers gloried in multiplying and
extending the visible signs of grief. On the
death of the Earl of Haddington, in 1643, his
chamber was " hung with mourneing " ; and
five years later there were not only a " black
cloath " bed, with tester, valance and curtains,
and chair and stool covers to correspond, but
also black baize hangings for the rooms, black
covers for the forms and other seats, and black
horse-cloths and liveries. Nothing was left un-
done to emphasise the most dismal aspects of
death and to aggravate the depressing circumstances of the bereaved. It is even said that
the mistress of Brunston had a particular alley
in her garden which she set aside for walking in
during mourning.

The furnishing of a four-poster in Queen
Mary's time consisted of (1) the covering, or
bed-cover ; (2) the headpiece or pane, rising
from the head of the bed ; (3) the roof or
canopy ; (4) three pands, forming the valance
or frieze-like hanging at the top of the curtains ;
(5) the curtains ; (6) the stoup-covers, the
material fitted round the bedposts, usually
wound spirally ; and (7) the underpands or
" subbasmont," hanging from the bed to the
floor. The top of the bed was often decorated
with " standardis of fedderis " at the four

corners, while in 1634 a citizen of Aberdeen had his bed similarly surmounted with no fewer than six tin crowns ! As to curtains, there is a set at present on view at the Royal Scottish Museum, on loan from Sir Charles Bruce, of Arnot, which are believed to have been hung on Queen Mary's bed during her imprisonment at Lochleven.[1] They are certainly of that date and they have many points of interest. They are of crimson cloth divided by broad bands of *appliqué* velvet embroidered in gold and colours. The curtains are four in number, besides the valances. When they came to the Museum they were measured, and it was found that while the height was approximately uniform— about 6 ft.—the width of the separate pieces was remarkably different, one being 44 in. wide, one 58 in., one 79 in., and the last as much as 99 in. Curtains are of course meant to hang with a certain amount of fullness, so they need not be expected to correspond precisely to the measurements of the bed. The proper arrangement seems to be this : the 58 in. one is the head-piece ; the shortest of all, that measuring 44 in., hangs next to the head on the side on which the bed was entered ; the 79 in. one hangs along the whole of the opposite side of the bed ; and the 99 in. one extends from that side along the foot of the bed and up the other side till it meets the short one, the meeting-place

[1] See Plate XII.

PLATE X

BED-CURTAINS FROM LOCH LEVEN
Property of Sir Charles Bruce of Arnot

occurring just where it would be most convenient that there should be an opening for
entering and leaving the bed. When the curtains at the Museum were arranged in this way
it was found that the edges of the curtains at
this opening were worn—perhaps by Queen
Mary's own hand as she drew them back to face
each new morning of her capitivity. The curtains show a characteristic feature of the beds
of the time, the strings and " knoppis " for
tying the curtains from inside before going to
sleep.

Heraldic ornament was often applied to beds,
either in the form of wood-carving, or executed
in needlework on the valance, head or coverlet.
But its appearance in private houses is rare
before the seventeenth century. David Wedderburn, the Dundee merchant, speaks, in 1622, of
" ane lite camp bed with my father and motheris
airmes thairon." Sir Colin Campbell, the
eighth Laird of Glenurquhy, who had a taste
for magnificence in furnishing, had one silk bed
with red hangings, " ane pand with rid velvett
brouderit with blew silk, with the Laird of
Glenurquhy and his Ladie their names and
airmes thairon." And other beds, one of blue,
one " incarnatt," and one of shot green and
yellow, similarly bore the arms of the laird and
his lady. The taste of the time seems to have
favoured such bright colours as these, and an

inventory of 1622 permits us a chaste glimpse of Mr. Adam Primrose, a native of Culross, retiring to his slumbers under the glowing shade of " orang growgrane courtenis." But, whether as a result of Puritan influence or no, these cheerful hues soon began to lose favour, and such romantic colour-names as crammasie and color-de-roy passed out of fashion. In their place we have a number of unpleasant names like " hair-cullour " and " flesche collor," and depressing ones like " sadd cullor " and " lead colour "; while there are also names, more attractive in themselves, which none the less stand for dull and neutral shades of various kinds, such as " gridaline " (*gris de lin*), a pinkish grey ; " gingalyne," ginger coloured ; and the pretty name " philiamort " (*feuille mort*) or dead leaf colour. Such colours taken as representative of the time convey an impression of an age which has lost much of the gaiety and romance of the fifteenth and sixteenth centuries. Yet on similar evidence what judgment would the archæologists of the future pass on our own time, for if we may trust the advertisements in to-day's papers the palette of the twentieth century would appear to be laid in with such mysterious shades as " nigger, putty, jade, bottle, tango and saxe " ?

LECTURE VI

THE COMMONWEALTH AND THE RESTORATION

1649–1688

The restoration of the Monarchy—Irreconcilable differences—Organised and harmonious national life impossible—Persecutions—The Acts of Indulgence—Inducements to accept the established regime—History of the times reflected in furniture—Severe and utilitarian character of Commonwealth furniture—Restoration chairs and daybeds—Chairs as evidences of changes in the treatment of floors—Easy chairs—Extravagance of the Court—Exotic materials—Cabinets—The chest of drawers—Tea, coffee and cocoa—Walnut tables—The virginalls—Barred grates—Forks not yet in use—Scottish diarists—Social life of the time—Billiards—Horse racing—The kirk stool—Going to church—Giving out the line—The hour-glass—Periwigs, powder and Sedan chairs, as preluding the eighteenth-century—Conclusion.

THE tragic course of Scottish history under the later Stuart kings resulted from the irreconcilable antagonism of two ideas, each entertained as a principle absolute and admitting of no compromise. On the one side, the people, with every fibre hardened in its long struggle for religious liberty, held unflinchingly to the divine right of conscience. On the other, the Royalists asserted no less peremptorily the divine right of Kings. The people's claim meant in practice the divine

173

authority of the Presbyterian form of religion. And as the King, in his capacity as Heaven's vice-regent, claimed the right to impose whatever form of religion commended itself to him, and as that form was not Presbyterianism, there was no possibility of a compromise such as might have led to a peaceful and harmoniously organised national life. For eleven years under the Commonwealth and Protectorate, Scotland had experienced, for the first time in her history, the domination of a foreign government whose rule was orderly and not unjust, but which was yet in many respects uncongenial. And when, in 1660, Charles II was restored to the throne, there were many whose experience of the form of government set up by the Covenant led them to accept with relief the return of the monarchy, and who looked hopefully forward to happier times under the ancient line of Scottish kings.

But it soon appeared that the old antagonism was to find no pacific solution, and that the policy of the King and his advisers aimed at nothing less than the total extirpation of the Covenant, a policy which would have been impracticable had not the nobility turned Royalist and had not the Covenanters themselves been divided by internal differences. The Recissory Act cancelled everything in the way of legislation that the Covenant had accomplished, and Presbyterian ministers had to forfeit their charges unless they brought themselves to apply for collation by a bishop. There followed the long story of persecution which has been described as " the most pitiful, the most revolting, and at the same time the sublimest and most impressive page in the national history." When we read the narrative of the torturings and the violent deaths of those who remained faithful to the Covenant and who refused to accept episcopacy and thus acknowledge Charles as the head of the Church, and when we contrast their sufferings with the untroubled existence that was open to them as an alternative, we cannot wonder if the majority were ready to compromise and purchase peace and immunity on easy terms, nor if many of the Presbyterian ministers took advantage of the Acts of Indulgence to regain possession of their charges. While the dragoons were scouring the moors and hillsides for the followers of Cargill, Cameron and Renwick, and the heather was stained with the blood of the martyrs, many an amiable country gentleman was peacefully attending to the management of his estates, and had most of his time free for the comparatively arduous pursuit of his pleasures. One would never suspect, from reading the Account Books of Sir John Foulis, of Ravelston, that he lived through a time whose tragedies have stamped themselves so deeply on Scottish memory. The same skies, the same alternations of rain and sunshine, saw the Covenanters exiled from human society, upheld through danger and privation by dark sayings of the Hebrew poets, and stung by their sufferings to an exaltation that was either prophecy or frenzy; and Foulis, in the friendliest good humour, making himself popular at horse races and penny weddings, dispensing drink-money to the midwife, and tossing a hansell with a kind word to " ye muckman that dights ye close."

Such antitheses could of course be drawn in our own or any age. Yet the contrasted pictures of the Covenanter and of the cheerful laird may serve to remind us of the alternatives that a man had to face when he resolved to stand by the Covenant, and of the inducement to swallow his qualms and choose the side of comfort and safety.

In the furnishing of the times it is possible to trace some reflexion of the events, the changes of national feeling, and the social contrasts, of which I have reminded you. Looking back to the previous reign we note that Charles I had been himself something of a collector and a patron of the arts, and his influence and example had had their effect in diffusing among the upper classes an interest in the furnishing of their homes. But with his death and the establishment of the Commonwealth there was a marked reaction, under Puritan influence, against ostentation and display, and a general reversion towards simplicity and even austerity in the whole setting of domestic life. The eleven years of the Commonwealth were too short a period to bring about any far-reaching change in the development of furniture, yet all the characteristic pieces of furniture which we associate with Cromwell's time are distinguished by their simple design, aiming at usefulness rather than comfort or ornament. Many of them were of earlier origin, types selected owing to their being naturally suited to the ascetic views of life and of human requirements which guided the Puritan's choice. Thus what is known as the Cromwell chair, a simple rectangular chair with a horizontal panel for the shoulders to rest on, and with the seat and panel covered with stretched leather nailed to the frame, was really a development of the " farthingale chair," the earliest armless form of chair, which was introduced in James VI's reign to meet the necessity of ladies who found that the enormous whalebone farthingales, or crinolines, then worn, were a source of embarrassment when they were given an arm-chair to sit on. In Cromwell's day the extremely narrow seat of the farthingale chair had been extended to a more comfortable size, and the legs and stretchers were often turned in a

12

" knob " pattern, though the straight leg was still perhaps more usual. On such chairs it was hardly possible to sit otherwise than bolt upright, so that there was little temptation to idle lounging. In the same way the gate-legged tables and writing bureaux of the period are furniture of a plain and homely type, such as men who aimed at sitting lightly to the world and its vanities might use without danger of having the eye seduced or the heart entangled.

After eleven years' experience of Puritan severity and repression, it was inevitable that there should be a revolt against a system that made little allowance for the natural instinct for beauty and innocent enjoyment. In Scotland especially, where the national struggle had never been directed against monarchical government, but merely against interference with religious liberty, the restoration of the Stuarts was hailed by most as a return of the good old times. Something of these feelings is crystallised in a very familiar type of contemporary furniture. What is often called a " Queen Mary chair," probably because of its association with Holyrood and also, perhaps, because the crown which is its characteristic decoration somewhat resembles the initial " M," is typical of the Restoration period.[1] The crown is no merely conventional piece of decoration, but expressly commemorates the return of the

[1] See Plate XIII.

(a)   (b)

CROWN CHAIRS
(<i>a</i>) PROPERTY OF SIR JOHN STERLING MAXWELL, BART.
(<i>b</i>) WITH THISTLE DECORATION, HOLYROOD PALACE (<i>Copyright of His Majesty the King</i></p>

monarchy; and in days when Royalist sympathies were not only naturally widespread but were also paraded, and sometimes perhaps even simulated, in order to allay suspicion of any Covenanting leanings, we need not be surprised that furniture that testified to one's loyalty had a considerable vogue. In those days, we are told, a solemn face was apt to prejudice a man's reputation, and a loud laugh was sedulously cultivated; so that Royalist furniture, besides being fashionable, had a precautionary value that appealed to the discreet. One characteristic feature of these chairs is the carved band which connects the front legs, and here, as on the top of the chair-back, the crown appears between two S-shaped scrolls or, in more elaborate examples, between two flying cherubs. The liberation from the severity of Puritan ideas is shown by the disappearance of straight legs and stretchers, and the knobbed turning of the late Commonwealth develops into " barley-sugar " spirals. The back has often a central panel, either rectangular or oval, which, like the seat, is stretched with trellised cane. The introduction of cane from the Malay Peninsula about this time was no doubt due to the East India Company, and Samuel Pepys first mentions it just after the Restoration, the entry being a rather characteristic one—" This morning, sending the boy down into the cellar for some beer

I followed him with a cane, and did there beat him for   his faults, and his sister came to me down and begged for him. So I forbore. . . and did talk to Jane how much I did love the boy for her sake." The early cane seats had a wider mesh than is now usual, and as they wore out they were often replaced by padded seats, the backs being similarly treated. Other chairs of this type have wavy splats in the back instead of cane. Chairs of the same character are also found in France, but the crown, which had not there the same significance, is less prominent and appears rather as a conventional ornament. In English chairs a rose often occurs between the pair of scrolls which decorates each side of the back panel, while at Holyrood there is a chair in which the thistle is conspicuously used.[1] In the later patterns we sometimes find the scroll form of leg—a form imported from France and destined to develop into the cabriole leg with which we are familiar in eighteenth-century furniture.

Another piece of furniture which is decorated with the crown is the day bed, generally called in Scotland the " resting " or " reposing bed." The day bed, which was the forerunner of the modern sofa, was known in Elizabethan times, and is, indeed, mentioned by Shakespeare. It was only after the Restoration, however, that it came into common domestic use, and it was a

[1] See Plate XIII.

considerable addition to the comfort of the hitherto scantily furnished drawing-rooms of the time. Like the chairs, these resting beds stood on spiral legs connected with spiral stretchers, and they had the carved band showing the crown and scrolls in front. The seat was covered in cane. At one end was a back intended to support the shoulders, and the inclination of this back could be varied and fixed by strings to the uprights. The back and the long seat were furnished with bright-coloured cushions, and altogether the resting bed was a picturesque and characteristic piece of furniture. It marks, perhaps, the beginning of the propensity to lounging which inspires so much of our modern furniture and makes the club smoking-room the paradise of the lethargic sprawler. The day bed, as a concession to human indolence, was accompanied by the sleeping-chair,[1] a good example of which may be seen at Holyrood. It is comfortably up-holstered and the back has a projecting wing at each side, so as to form corners in which it was possible to dose with the head supported and sheltered from draughts. Notice, as a feature which this chair shares with the crown and other contemporary types of chair, the carved band which connects the front legs some way from the ground. As long as rushes were in use for covering floors, it was practically im-

[1] See Plate XIV.

possible to keep floors sweet and clean, and much unsavoury debris of one kind and another was apt to accumulate. The chairs and tables of those days accordingly show a plain stretcher near the ground on which the feet could be supported and kept clear of the floor. But when rushes gave place to carpets or to bare floors, which are often shown in seventeenth-century prints, the low stretcher had become an encumbrance which prevented people from tucking their feet below their chairs if they wished to do so. The stretcher, which strengthened the chair by binding the front legs together, was therefore raised, and, being no longer exposed to wear and tear from human heels, it developed into a decorative feature and was enriched with carving. How elaborate this carved decoration became may be seen in the double chair, also at Holyrood, which bears a ducal coronet and a monogram embroidered on the back of each seat. It appears to date from about 1680.

There are many influences other than the mere reaction against Puritanism which must be taken into account in tracing the development of furniture after the Restoration. One of these is the re-establishment of the Court, which was a powerful factor in diffusing extravagant habits of living. Charles himself, during his residence in France and Holland,

PLATE X

SLEEPING CHAIR, HOLYROOD PALACE
Copyright of His Majesty the King

had become familiar with more luxurious standards than those that had been countenanced under the Commonwealth ; and, as Evelyn tells us, " he brought in a politer way of living, which passed to luxury and intolerable expense." Were it necessary to illustrate the extent of the reaction at Court against the austere standards of Puritanism one might quote Evelyn's picture of the Court as he saw it within a week before the death of Charles II : " I can never forget the inexpressible luxury and profaneness, gaming and all dissoluteness, and as it were total forgetfulness of God (it being Sunday evening) which this day sennight I was witness of ; the King sitting and toying with his concubines, Portsmouth, Cleveland and Mazarin, etc., a French boy singing love-songs in that glorious gallery, while about twenty of the great courtiers and other dissolute persons were at basset round a large table, a bank of at least two thousand pounds in gold before them ; upon which two gentlemen who were with me made reflections with astonishment. Six days after, was all in the dust."

In much of the furniture of the period the tendency to ostentatious display is plainly enough shown. There was a return from Puritan sobriety to the use of rich and brilliant colours in covering chairs, as well as in cushions and curtains. Some of the ladies whose names have just been quoted, and others whose names are equally familiar in connection with the scandals of the Court, exercised a distinct influence in this direction and had their part in the movement which brought into fashion all sorts of tinselled fringes, tassels and borders. The same tendency was shown by the introduction of such materials as ebony, tortoiseshell, ivory and mother-of-pearl, and their application to coffers and cabinets and other furniture. Charles had probably some experience of the use of these eastern substances during his exile in Holland ; and they were brought to England by the English East India Company, which, incorporated by Queen Elizabeth in 1600, was so prosperous in Charles II's reign that one shareholder sold out his two hundred and fifty pounds of stock to the Royal Society for seven hundred and fifty pounds, a transaction which he describes as " extraordinary advantageous, by the blessing of God." Some of the furniture with ivory or mother-of-pearl inlay has a distinctly Saracenic suggestion, and it is likely that this may have come through Portugal as a result of Charles's marriage with Catherine of Bragança. To the disappointment of the King, his bride's dowry was paid in kind and not in cash. It included, besides sugar and spices, a considerable quantity of furniture which naturally gave a turn to the fashions of the time. The Bragança " toe " is a familiar type in furniture to this. day. Even more important as an influence than the furniture was the cession to England, under the marriage treaty, of Tangier and especially of Bombay, which was the first step towards the acquisition of her eastern imperial possessions.

The exotic materials that have been mentioned were freely employed in the decoration of the cabinets which are a feature of the Restoration period. The word was applied not, as in our time, to large armoires and cupboards, but particularly to comparatively small chests of coffers supported on stands and containing a number of drawers. Such pieces were not unknown in the sixteenth century, and, indeed, Queen Mary had one which is described as " ane cabinet lyke ane coffer coverit with purpour velvet, quhairin is drawin litil buists to keip writtingis in." But since Mary's day the habit of writing and the number of confidential documents had greatly increased. Correspondence must have reached a considerable volume since the Union of the Crowns. In 1635 Charles I had inaugurated the inland post " to run night and day between Edinburgh and London, to go thither and come back again in six days, and to take with them all such letters as shall be directed to any post town in or near that road " It was sixty years later before the

internal postal communications in Scotland
were taken in hand by the Scottish Parliament.
But the amount of correspondence was enough
to explain the demand for cabinets. The
religious diaries too of which we have spoken
were presumably kept under lock and key, for
it is one thing for a man to humble himself
before his Maker and quite another thing to
tell the story of his lapses and shortcomings to
the peeping Toms, the prying Dicks and the
gossiping Harrys of his own household, to say
nothing of their feminine counterparts. Such
considerations and the secrets contained in
letters at a time when the whole kingdom was
so divided on questions of religion and politics,
and when so many people for one reason and
another changed sides, explain also the introduction of sliding panels and secret drawers
whose use was so highly developed in the
cabinets of the Restoration. Of these the
Lennoxlove Cabinet[1] is a good type. It is described in an early inventory as " The Duchess's
Cabinet," and it is said to have been presented
by Charles II to Frances Theresa Stuart,
Duchess of Lennox, known as " la belle Stuart."
The convex hearts of red tortoise-shell have
thus a special significance. If the outside of
the cabinet, with its inlays and applications of
various ornamental materials, is characteristic,
so also is the inside with its many drawers

[1] See Plate XV.

EBONY AND TORTOISE-SHELL CABINET (CHARLES II) AT LENNOXLOVE
Property of Major W. A. Baird

and hidden receptacles. The word " cabinet " means of course a little house, and it is interest ing to note the tradition of architectural treat- ment which they exemplify. In this cabinet, as in so many others, the central recess is flanked by columns, and its floor is inlaid with black and white squares, like the portico of some great building.

An Act of James VI " Anent Banqueting and Apparel " had forbidden the use of gold and silver lace on apparel, " embroydering or any lace or passements upon cloathes, and pearling or ribbening upon ruffles, sarkes, napkins and sockes." It had even attempted to perpetuate the " fashion of Cloathes now presently used." But by Charles II's time such restrictions, as well as those imposed by Puritanism, had been forgotten, and dress was both gay and elaborate. What with silk brocades, lace, silver edgings, embroidered belts and all the other fineries of the day it was found necessary to devise a piece of furniture more convenient than the old chest or the shelved aumrie, in which such things could be kept accessible, free from dust and arranged in some kind of order. The first step was to add a couple of drawers side by side in the lower part of the chest ; and gradually the number of drawers was increased, till the hinged lid gave place to a fixed top and the whole of the accommodation was devoted to drawers.

Thus was evolved that modern and convenient piece of bedroom furniture the " chest of drawers," which is what its name literally implies, though not in the too literal sense in which an Englishman is said to have asked in a French shop for a *poitrine de caleçons*. The chest in its original form was now superseded and for practical purposes ceased to be made. The new form was similar in idea to the cabinets described above, and in the earlier specimens the drawers, or at least the upper drawers, were often enclosed by a pair of doors opening in the centre.

Those were days in which a great deal of liquor was drunk and drink-money was distributed lavishly to thirsty dependents on all sorts of occasions. But thanks once more to the East India Company tea and coffee began to come into use in England about 1660, while chocolate was also introduced, and we find allusions to the use of these beverages in Scotland not many years later. At first they were looked upon as having a certain medicinal virtue, being recommended for the " defluxions," but they soon won their way on their merits as beverages and began to bring about social changes. Tea and coffee houses sprang up, and there men foregathered to read the news sheets and to play cards and other games of chance and skill, so that there was soon an increased demand for small folding tables, often made of walnut—a wood which, being of more even texture than oak, was a more satisfactory material for the spiral legs favoured by the taste of the time. The employment of walnut and the discovery of its special qualities by the workmen who handled it led to the development of a lighter and more graceful type of furniture than the cumbrous oak furniture of earlier times, just as the introduction of mahogany in the following century led to further progress towards the ideal of slender and sometimes rather flimsy elegance.

The introduction of these folding tables and of furniture of a comparatively light kind, which could be easily moved from one part of a room to another, and the gradual adoption of tea and coffee, and many other small changes of habits, served cumulatively to bring a more modern atmosphere into the domestic life of the time. There was also a considerable development of the taste for music in private houses. Young ladies were taught to play the viol and the virginals, to the pride of their parents and, let us hope, to the satisfaction of less partial listeners. The charming pair of virginals shown in Plate XVI is a good specimen of the instruments on which they performed. It has spiral legs corresponding to those of the chairs and tables of the time. The keys, instead of being faced with ivory, are of solid boxwood, which was the material used for that purpose in Charles II's reign, and they are worn with the touch of slender fingers which made music two hundred and fifty years ago. The compass is only about four and a half octaves, and the tone was sweet and delicate, not powerful and sonorous like our modern pianos with their massive iron frames and their heavily loaded wires stretched at enormous tension. At each end of the keyboard is a little carved figure, and one cannot but feel that this instrument, if less efficient, is at least in outward form much more charming and sympathetic to the artist than the French-polished and stony-hearted looking monsters which are its modern descendants. The fifth, or central, leg seems to be an eighteenth century addition designed to carry a lever operated by a pedal for the purpose of opening and closing the lid in order to increase or diminish the volume of tone. The expression "pair of virginals" does not, of course, denote two instruments, but merely refers to the series of notes, as in old times a rosary was called a "pair of beads," or as we still talk of a "pair of stairs."

One other change contributed to the modern air of the houses of the period—the introduction of barred grates in place of the old open fireplace. In the engravings of Abraham Bosse,

VIRGINALS (CHARLES II)
Property of Miss Simpson, Edinburgh

who was born about 1610, and whose works are full of interest as pictures of seventeenth-century life, the fireplaces are open and fitted with a pair of andirons to support the fuel. The early Scottish grate was called a chimney, and it was fitted with a pair of " raxis," either standing or lying ; it had an iron back and at the side there was often fitted a " gallows " with crooks or chains, from which a pot could be hung. The customary fireside implements were a " porring irne," or poker, and a pair of tongs. The " foreface," with ribs, was introduced before 1660, and we read in Lamont of Newton's *Diary* in 1661 that " The Lady caused make a new chemnay for the hall of Lundy, of the newest fashion with long bars of iron before, with a high backe, all of iron behind." Grates of this type may still be seen in Holyrood, which was restored and furnished for Charles II in the years following 1671, though those actually in use are reproductions of the originals still on view.

Before passing on to a sketch of the social life of the time, let me say a few words on a subject on which, in my earlier lectures, I have only touched in a negative sense—I mean the question of the use of forks at table. We have seen that a single fork was occasionally used for handling fruit, and that the luxurious Parson of Stobo had one of these rarities in the earlier half of the sixteenth century. In *Coryat's Crudities*, published in 1611, the author writes of the use of forks in cutting meat as a curious custom which he had seen in his travels, " neither doe I thinke that any other nation of Christendome doth use it, but only Italy. . . . The reason of this their curiosity is, because the Italian cannot by any means endure to have his dish touched with fingers, seeing all men's fingers are not alike cleane." A character in Ben Jonson's comedy, *The Devil is an Ass*, exclaims, " Forks ? What be they ? " and receives this answer ·

> The laudable use of forks,
> Brought into custom here, as they are in Italy,
> To th' sparing o' napkins.

But, though the custom would thus seem to have been introduced early in the seventeenth century, it appears to have died out both in England and in France. The explanation may perhaps be found in the fact that they were found useful at the time when wide ruffs, worn round the neck, made it difficult to reach the mouth with the hand ; so that when ruffs passed out of fashion the use of forks was discontinued. In France the practice reappeared among the fashionable and fastidious in the latter half of the seventeenth century, on the initiative, it is said, of the Duc de Montausier ; and a French " Traité de Civilité " exhorts well-bred persons " porter la viande à la bouche·

avec sa fourchette." In spite of this there is abundance of evidence that even in important French houses food continued to be lifted with the fingers, and it was apparently only in the eighteenth century that the use of forks was established as a general practice. Certainly within Stuart times, to which my own researches have hitherto been confined, I have found no instance of a supply of forks for table use in Scotland ; and the large numbers of napkins inventoried in Scottish houses support the view that meat was still handled as in mediæval times. It may, however, be noted that when, in 1669, Charles II entertained Cosimo II, Duke of Tuscany, knives and forks were laid for the guests, and there may have been houses where the practice was adopted before it became a usual one.

A curious point about table knives may be added. These, as early illustrations show, used to have sharp points, as penknives still have ; and sharp points must have had many practical advantages. Why, then, have our modern table knives rounded points ? The change took place in France in the first half of the seventeenth century, when Cardinal Richelieu, disgusted at Chancellor Séguier's gross habit of picking his teeth with the point of his knife, a habit which was no doubt common enough, had the points of his table knives rounded to prevent

13

the recurrence of so offensive a spectacle. The fashion thus set was generally adopted ; and in dissecting the wing of a chicken with a round-pointed knife one may console oneself with the reflection that one suffers vicariously for the solecism of a Chancellor of France.

I suppose there is no epoch of English history of whose social and domestic life we have such brilliant and intimate glimpses as Pepys' immortal *Diary* gives us of the period of the Restoration. In Scotland we have nothing comparable to that sparkling and outspoken journal. Law's *Memorials* give many interesting sidelights on the ecclesiastical and political affairs of the time. Lamont, of Newton, records with impartial fidelity the meetings of Fifeshire Presbyteries and the winners of the Cupar horse races. Neither writer has the English diarist's genius for jotting down vividly and with unflagging zest the trifling yet enthralling incidents of his daily life. It is only occasionally that such writers are surprised into an unconventional note, as when Lamont writes, " Sept. 6, being Saturn's day, the garner's mother in Balcarresse was bitten through the arme with a puggy ther, which did blood so therafter that it could not be stem'd. Some few days therafter she dyed." Of all our diarists of that time Lauder, of Fountainhall, has the most alert observation and the wittiest tongue. Of a bad crossing to France he writes, " What a distressed brother I was upon the sea neids not hear be told. . . . Mr. John Kincead and I strove who should have the bucket first, both being equally ready. . . . At every gasp he gave he cried God's mercy, as if he had been to expire immediately." Arrived in France, which he hails as the land " of graven images," he is " not a little amazed to see upright poddock stools " being prepared for his diet. Of these the Scot partakes without enthusiasm, yet he owns that " in eating them a man seimes to be iust eating of tender collops." Another experience of French cookery, in which the legs of a frog were substituted for those of a pullet, drives him to exclaim, " Such damnd cheats be all the French ! " He is far too canny to admit prematurely any good opinion of those he meets, even if they are fellow Scots. " The Mr. of Ogilvie and I were very great," he says ; but adds, " I know not what for a man he'el prove, but I have heard him talk wery fat nonsense whiles." He husbands his expletives to impart a sting to his observations on men and things which are not of his own country. Thus he introduces an anecdote of the patron Saint of Ireland with the remark, " The Irishes hes a damned respect for St. Phatrick." If Lauder's gift of racy expression had been transferred to **Foulis,** of Ravelston, and had been devoted to

keeping a journal of his occupations and amusements, we might have had something like a
Scottish Pepys. But Foulis's doings have to
be dug out of his Account Books. There we
can trace a round of duties and pleasures that
might have supplied material for a delightful
diary ; how he went to Cramond to fish and to
Lothianburn to hunt, or how a less cheerful
errand took him to Mr. Strachan, the watch-
maker in the Canogait, to have a new tooth
fitted to its place with silk. Leith appears to
have been the Elysium frequented by those who
cultivated sport and the drama ; to Leith the
Laird of Fountainhall made frequent expedi-
tions to see a horse race or to play a round of
golf ; and to Leith he would convey a party to
see a comedy—*The Spanish Curate*, or *The
Silent Woman*—and would not forget to treat
the ladies during the performance to cherries or
oranges. These entries give us a picture of a
cheerful Scottish laird, attending to his estates
and the upkeep of his house, a welcome figure
whether in patronising a penny wedding or in
" conveying Lady Kimmergem's corps " ; taking in hand the family shopping, buying a golf
club to Archie, Rudiments to Jonie and a pair
of strait sleeves to Lissie, as well as five ells of
stringing for " hangers to hys own breeches " ;
and at the same time, out of a kind heart and a
comfortable purse, dispensing rather indis-

criminate alms to " a poor irishman, he called himself foulis," " a distrest man named middle-toune wanting ye nose " and other casual applicants ; and then, perhaps in doubt as to the wisdom of his charity, paying an officer fourteen shillings Scots " to keep away ye poor." If he has many a festive evening and loses many a wager at golf or cards, he is willing that his family too should amuse themselves, and he leaves two pounds with his " douchter Jean to give the fidler and play at cards." Like that hero of song, Captain Wattle, who " was all for love, and a little for the bottle," he sets small store by literature, science, or the arts. Public affairs receive little of his attention, though when the future James VII visited Scotland in pursuit of the anti-Covenanter measures, he makes it an excuse for another jaunt to Leith, where he hires a boat " to see the duke of york go abord-o "—the entry having a quasi-nautical turn which suggests that he enjoyed his day and came home pleasantly exhilarated.

A good deal of light is thrown on the social habits of the day in connection with births, marriages and deaths. On the death of Sir John's first wife, a lad was sent round with intimations sealed in black to the houses of the neighbouring lairds. The house at Ravelston was hung with black serge, the church pew was covered with the same material, and Meg,

Lissie and Grissie were provided with black
" under pitticoats." The widower himself re-
quires a yard and a half of black looping for his
hat and hatband, a pair of black shoe-buckles
and a mourning sword, while his horse has to
be arrayed in black trappings. The funeral
charges include the " dead chist " and " sear
cloathes," the cost of " embowelling my dear
wife," and fees to bellmen, trumpeters and the
cryer, the keepers of the mortcloath, and the
herald-painter who provided the hatchment
placed on the front of the house to announce
the quality of the dead lady. Within two
months all these bills had been paid, and before
another two months had passed Sir John seems
to have forgotten the mother of his fourteen
children and is once more a bridegroom, wearing silver buckles and garters, paying for an
epithalamium and calling once more on the
trumpeters, to play this time at his wedding.
Such swift remarriage does not seem to have
been considered disrespectful to the memory of
the first wife. A man, William Lundin, in Fife,
married as his second wife Helen Lithell, and we
are told that " the said Helen Lithell was
spoken of at the tabell of Lundin one day att
dinner before that the deceaset Elspet Adie, his
first wife, was interred, to be a fitt woman for
his second wife." Apparently he should have
waited till a few days after the funeral. Fortu-

nately native caution prevented many men from running too hastily into matrimony. A plough-man was asked by the Presbytery of Elgin why he had changed his mind after proclamation of banns, and gave four good reasons for his having declined the venture : " 1. He could not get his parents' consent. 2. He could not get his master's consent. 3. The wumman was lous fingered. 4. They promised him 100 merks and could nor wald pay it."

Among Sir John Foulis's recreations, billiards is not named, yet it is likely enough that he may have known the game. Though it is men-tioned by Spenser and Shakespeare, billiards seems only to have been made fashionable by Louis XIV in the middle of the seventeenth century, and it is all the more remarkable to find that there was " ane old spoyld bulliert boord " in the West Gallery at Birsay House, Orkney, so early as 1653. Kirk, who visited Scotland in 1677, mentions the game as taking up part of his time at Aberdeen. There were, of course, many on the Crown as well as on the Covenant side who disapproved of such recrea-tions as billiards, cards and horse racing ; and an easygoing father sometimes incurred severe criticism from his own straitlaced offspring. It is plain that the Earl of Rothes combined affection for his daughter the Countess of Haddington with a wholesome dread of her austere standards of conduct, as the following letter to his son-in-law will show ·

"Thursday, wan a cklok.

My Dear Lord,

All that cips runieng horsics in Scotland being jeust going to diner with me, I have taym onlie to tell you that Sir Andrew Ramsie and Poso runs on Satirday by aliuin a cklok, which will be a verie gret math, and I beliue much munie upon it ; and on Tyousday bothe the plet runs, at which ther is six horsics ; and Mortein's old hors and mayn runs a by mathe. This is onlie to inform you, not to inwayt you, for I dear not for my doghter ; but if you cum, which I wold du if I uere in your ples, you shall be verie velcum to your

R.

My seruies to my dear Maig, and all the rest of your good cumpanie.

For the Earle of Haddingtoune—these."

There is one piece of furniture which is often met with in seventeenth-century houses, whose use carries us beyond the limits of the house itself. This was the "kirk stuill." Even "kirk chairs" are mentioned, and these may have been of a folding type so as to make them easily carried. Usually, however, well-to-do people had their own pews for which they paid "dask maill" or pew rent, and it was only necessary to carry with them the cushions, generally covered in velvet, which gave a certain amount of alleviation while listening to the prolonged sermons of the time. The use of kirk cushions is mentioned as a new fashion in the middle of the sixteenth century in Maitland's *Satyre on the Town Ladies*, where he says :

> In kirk thai are not content of stuillis
> The sermon quhen they sit to heir,
> But caryis cuschingis lyike vaine fuillis
> And all for newfangilnes of geir.

In the seventeenth century many of the churches had still thatched roofs, and we read of some in country districts with " the doors sodded up and no windows." The kirk-brod or plate, stood at the door, or the collection might be taken by ladles. The church-goer prepared himself at home by wrapping his intended offering in his " nepeking end," that is, the corner of his handkerchief, so that he could lay hands upon it when wanted, and perhaps to prevent his putting in a coin of higher value by mistake. In some churches the tradesmen sat above in the pews allotted to the several trades, the gentlemen sat below, and the women in the " high end " or near the pulpit. When the minister prayed it was customary for the congregation to " use a hummering kind of lamentation for their sins," and this moaning and shuddering must have produced a curious and impressive effect. As to the singing, the custom of " giving out the line " was introduced about 1640 ; each line was chanted in monotone before the congregation sang it. Sometimes the effect of separating the lines in this way rather perplexed the sense. Thus in the verse beginning :

> I'll praise the Lord, and I will not
> Keep silence, but speak out.

the precentor intoned, in all solemnity, the words, " I'll praise the Lord and I will not," and this paradox was thereupon adopted unanimously by the loud-voiced congregation. Taking advantage of their docility the unreasonable precentor went on to chant, " Keep silence, but speak out ! " a command which the faithful flock echoed without a qualm.

On the pulpit was fixed a bracket containing an hour glass. As soon as the preacher had given out his text, the men put on their hats, the glass was turned and the sermon began and was seldom over before the sands had run out. Sometimes the preacher had periods of " desertion " in which even men like Thomas Boston " had much ado to see out the glass " ; and sometimes, on the other hand, congregations had to get their ministers restrained from habitually exceeding the time-limit. Generally the preachers seem to have taken a gloomy view of the probable fate of their hearers in the next world. In a Journal of the time we read of Mr. Rob. Wedderburn addressing his congregation thus : " God will even come over the hil at the back of the kirk their, and cry wt a hy voice, Angel of the church of Maln (moon) sy, compeir ! Then Ile answer, Lord behold thy servant, what hes thou to say to him ? Then God wil say, ' Wheir are the souls thou hest won by your ministry heir thir 17 years ? ' Ile no wal what to answer to this, for Sirs, I cannot promise God one of your souls : yet Ile say, Behold my own soul and my crooked Bessie's (this was his daughter) ; and wil not this be a sad matter ? "

For the writer of to-day, as for the preachers of forgotten yesterdays, the sands run low and time imposes inexorable limits. Were it permissible to view, as Moses did, the land which I must not enter and to look but a year or two beyond the date to which I have confined myself, we should find a new Foulis of Ravelston, no longer wearing his own hair and paying frequent visits to the barber's to have it trimmed, but decked with a periwig ; we should find that James Peacock has been called in to " cut and powder the bairns' hair," and that her ladyship is carried to her lodging in a Sedan chair. Such changes prelude the dawn of the eighteenth century, and, as students of the seventeenth, we may take a jealous satisfaction in believing that some of them at least were not endured without a pang. To take to a periwig called for considerable resolution. With one diarist the crisis of indecision and procrastination lasted for six months. When he first tried on a wig, he found that he had no stomach for it, " but that the paines of keeping my haire clean is so great." Some months passed, and he made another attempt, but again put it off for a while. More months slipped by, and then, taking the desperate plunge, he had his hair cut off, " which went a little to my heart at present to part with it." He adds somewhat ruefully, " But it is over, and so I perceive after two or three days it will be no great matter."

In our study of Domestic Life in Scotland we have had to consider many things which in themselves are of little importance—the setting of a salt-cellar, the lifting of a mouthful of food, the form of a table or chair. Yet such things are the footprints of our race on their long journey from primitive barbarism to the usages and conventions of a humaner civilisation. Step by step man has risen from a listless tenure of the cave and forest homes which he shared with the beasts; generation by generation he has wrought for himself a home reflecting his human desire not only for comfort and decency and order, but for kindly converse with his fellows, and at last also for beauty and the exercise and refreshment of the mind. And for us the story of his progress and the small things and tentative advances of his domestic life can never be trivial or insignificant.

But on the other hand our survey, in dealing with the little things and changing fashions of life and manners, and in recalling the swift succession of eager but transient generations, may—if we are to seek for a closing morality— fitly enough remind us also of the littleness of much that preoccupies the minds of men. If the putting on of a periwig marks and symbolises the end of an era, the wearer at least mourns the loss of his locks rather than the flight of the irredeemable years. Though he clings in his heart to old and familiar ways, the new mode is not to be resisted, and he accepts it with the best grace he can. Thus is human life tangled in the meshes of worldly mutability. Thus, amid the vagaries of ephemeral fashion and petty but perpetual change, do generations pass and epochs roll to their appointed close. Trifles press and encroach upon us ; meanwhile the morning is gone ere we know it, and evening already draws in. Life, with its romantic offers, comes and swiftly goes, opportunity flows by and is not to be won again. That fair white page, on which we had vowed but yesterday to inscribe deeds worth doing and not to be blotted out, is to-day scribbled and smirched with the record of our inconstant aims and fitful resolutions. Farewell to all we had hoped for, had counted on, yet had not the wit to sieze! Little wonder if it goes somewhat to our heart to part with it. Yet the world goes merrily on. The virtues we might have won hard in life are freely given us in an epitaph; and those who follow after us are busy already with the cakes and ale. Of all our laborious trifling, what remains? Have we added a single stone to that shining Temple which it is the task of the ages to uprear? Who can say? The issues of human effort are beyond human disposal. Yet if a man have learned wisdom, if, losing all things, he have won the grace of a humble spirit, he may look back at the last on all he had hoped and the little he has done, and may say without bitterness in his heart, " It is over; and so I perceive after two or three days it will be no great matter."

INDEX

Printed in Great Britain at
The Mayflower Press, Plymouth,
William Brendon & Son, Ltd.

CPSIA information can be obtained
at www.ICGtesting.com
Printed in the USA
LVOW04s1003240616

493972LV00012B/177/P